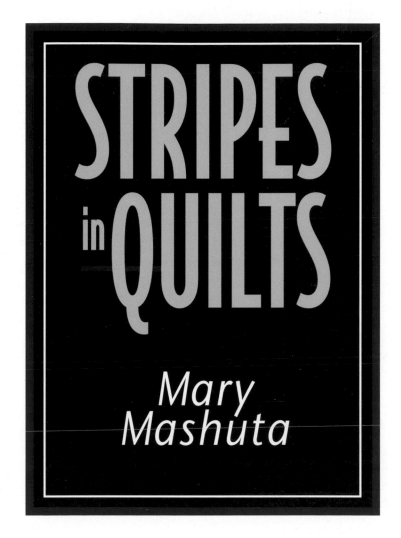

STRIPES in QUILTS

Mary Mashuta

C&T PUBLISHING

© Copyright 1996 Mary Mashuta

Developmental Editor: Barbara Konzak Kuhn
Technical Editor: Sally Lanzarotti
Book Design: Kajun Graphics, San Francisco, CA
Illustrator: Kandy Petersen, Moraga, CA
All photography by Sharon Risedorph unless otherwise noted.
Glued mock-ups designed by Mary Mashuta and made by Rebecca Rohrkaste, Angie Woolman, or Mary Mashuta unless otherwise noted.

ISBN 1-57120-008-8

Library of Congress Cataloging-in-Publication Data
Mashuta, Mary.
      Stripes in quilts/Mary Mashuta
              p. cm.
      ISBN 1-57120-008-8 (pbk.)
      1. Patchwork.   2. Machine quilting–Patterns.
      3. Patchwork quilts.   I. Title.
   TT835.M3843 1996
   746.46'.41--dc20   95-45012
                                CIP

Marimekko is a registered trademark of Marimekko Oy.
Nancy Crow for John Kaldor is a registered trademark of John Kaldor Fabricmaker.
Omnigrid is a registered trademark of Omnigrid Inc.
Sulky is a registered trademark of Sulky of America.

Published by C&T Publishing
P.O. Box 1456
Lafayette, California 94549

Printed in Hong Kong
10 9 8 7 6 5 4 3 2 1

To Daddy and Roberta for the gift of time...

To Rebecca, Angie, and Anne for the use of their hands when mine were not enough.

Table of Contents

Alhambra Olé, 47" x 47", Mary Mashuta, 1995; in the collection of P&B Textiles

Chapter 1
Let's Talk About Stripes

I think stripes are wonderful, but they are a category of pattern that is often ignored by quilters. Some quilters just don't buy them; others buy them, but don't use them; others use only one type; and still others buy all they can get their hands on and enjoy using them in their quilts. I belong to the latter group!

▤ *What Are Stripes?*
Stripes are a directional or linear pattern made up of straight lines running parallel to each other. I have adapted the definition to say that stripes are a linear pattern of more-or-less straight lines, or bands of design motifs, running more-or-less parallel to each other. (Since plaids have lines crossing or intersecting each other, they don't count as stripes.) Many quilters say they don't use stripes; however, they create their own homemade stripes every time they strip piece

fabrics together. Maybe we should think of striped fabrics as cheater cloth strip piecing. Imagine the time you could save if you bought and used a stripe, instead of taking the time to strip piece fabrics.

▤ *What Do Stripes Do in Quilts?*
The lines that stripes create usually catch the attention of the viewer. As the eye follows the stripe, the repetitiveness of the lines causes the eye to "trip along" or follow the repeating pattern to see where it is going. (Plaids have lines going both ways, so they trap and stop the eye.) Stripes also provide contrast to other print types to help make quilts more interesting. Some stripes demand attention and have to be the "stars" in the quilt. Others add interest and are important bit players, and still others are more demure and act as part of the chorus.

Woven stripes

▤ *Assessing Stripes*

The characteristics of an individual stripe pattern determine how pronounced its effect will be in a specific quilt. For this reason, you need to become familiar with the stripes before you cut the fabric.

Stripes are either woven into or printed onto the fabric. Most often the stripes are either parallel or perpendicular to the edge of the fabric. Occasionally, they are printed diagonally. Usually the right side of a printed stripe is used, but either side can be used if the stripes are woven.

The group of lines that make a striped fabric are arranged in either an even or uneven pattern. Deciding whether a stripe is even (balanced, symmetrical, regular) or uneven (unbalanced, asymmetrical, irregular) is very important.

Most stripes are vertical stripes because they run parallel to the selvage. If you are having trouble deciding whether a vertical stripe is even or uneven, first fold the fabric selvage to selvage with the right sides "kissing." (For a horizontal stripe, fold the fabric cut edge to cut edge.) Then, fold back a diagonal triangle and see if you can match the lines to form a chevron.

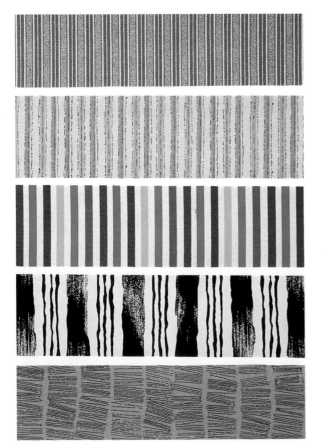

Printed stripes

Diagonal printed stripes

Even vertical stripe = lines on folded back triangle can form a chevron

Uneven vertical stripe = lines on folded back triangle can't form a chevron

If an even stripe is centered within a pattern piece, such as a sashing strip, you will end up with identical lines at both ends of the piece. If an uneven stripe is used, you can never end up with the lines being the same at the ends because the pattern reads in one direction only. You can use both even and uneven stripes, but it's best to know which one you have before you start your work.

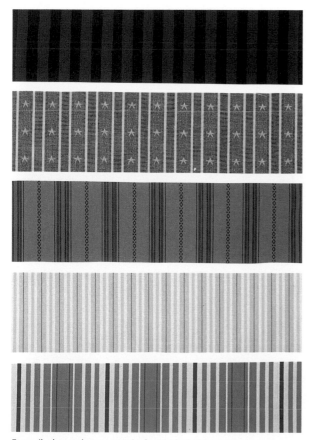

Even (balanced, symmetrical, regular) stripes

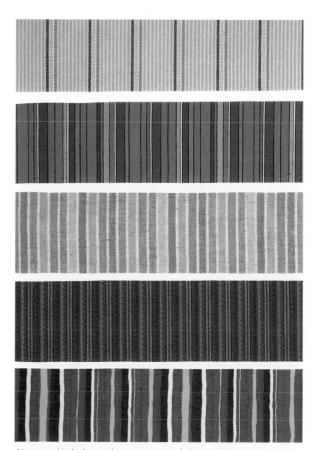

Uneven (unbalanced, asymmetrical, irregular) stripes

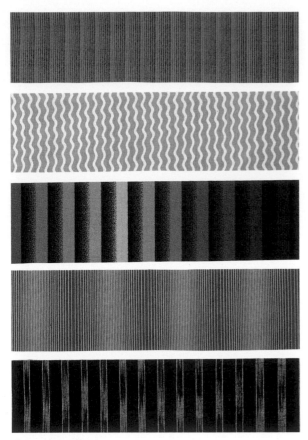

One-color stripes

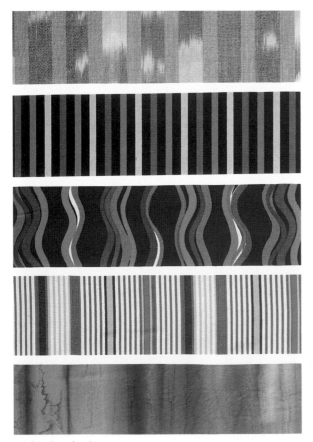

Multicolored stripes

Color

In addition to linear pattern, another characteristic that attracts me to stripes is their color. The number of colors in a stripe affects the activity level of the quilt.

Printed stripes and other patterned fabrics are often produced in different colorways, or color versions. (In this book, you will learn how to take advantage of this fact.) The manufacturer gets better mileage out of the pattern because there is expense involved in creating the original design and in engraving the plates. People may like the pattern but want other colors, so it makes sense to offer a variety of colors. Patterns that sell well are often repeated in later seasons in other colorways. Woven stripe patterns can also have other colors substituted to create different colorways.

I often use several color versions of the same stripe in a quilt. But, I first used two colorways of a fabric when I had run out of a fabric for my Persian Gulf quilt, *Lessons Learned* on page 17. (I guess I had originally purchased the other colorways because I didn't know how I would eventually use the fabric. I wanted to keep my options open when I added the fabric to my patriotic fabric collection.) I liked the end result when I substituted the other colorways. In fact,

Three colorways of one stripe pattern

the quilt was much more interesting. The next time I ran out of fabric, I knew that I might be able to substitute another colorway. Eventually I learned to always ask to see the other colorways.

Normally, quilters are attracted by color to quilts. Value contrast, or the difference between light and dark, helps you "read" the pattern within the colors. The value contrast in a stripe pattern makes the stripe stand out, or blend in, based on its color. Stripes with high value contrast demand attention.

Just as print fabrics are sometimes spotty (the print has lots of little motifs that contrast sharply against the background color on which they are placed), striped fabrics can be spotty, too. Some stripe patterns jump before your eyes because there is high contrast between the lines, the motifs, and the background.

Some people have a visual astigmatism. High contrast, small scale stripes distort, or jump around, as they look at them. Most of these people find they can work with softer, more muted stripes that have less contrast. If you are one of these people, avoid working with spotty stripes.

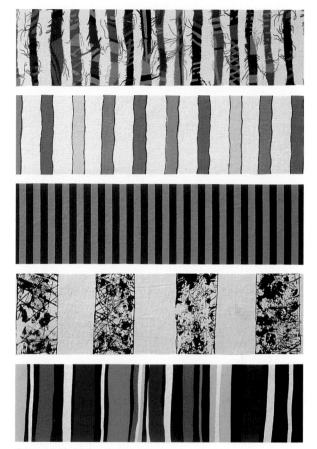

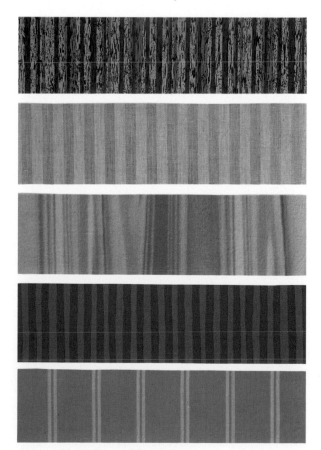

Stripes with high value contrast

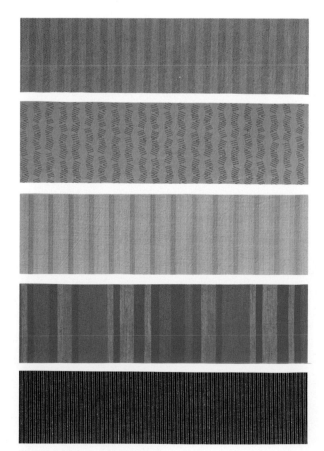

Stripes with low value contrast

Stripes with medium value contrast

9

▤ *Special Types of Stripes*

Some stripes aren't just ordinary stripes. They have qualities which make them unique.

Border prints can be classified as stripes only if enough of the pattern is used (when it is cut) so that it reads as a stripe from a distance.

Most stripes have absolutely straight and parallel lines, but the edges of some stripes vary slightly and appear somewhat wavy. These stripes look like they were drawn with a marking pen. You have the feeling someone created these stripes while he or she was doodling.

Paintbrush stripes are even more abstract than marker-drawn stripes. The stripes in these fabrics look as if they were painted with a brush.

Some woven stripes are also abstract. Ikat woven stripes have one of the sets of yarns partially dyed before they are woven. The color alignment isn't perfect so the lines become fuzzy. These stripes are so beautiful that manufacturer's have produced printed imitations.

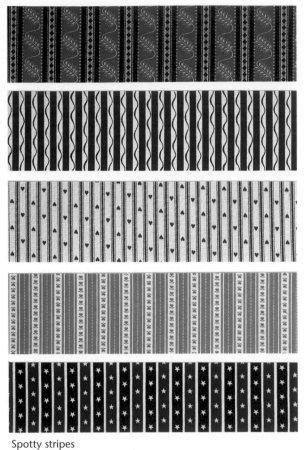

Spotty stripes

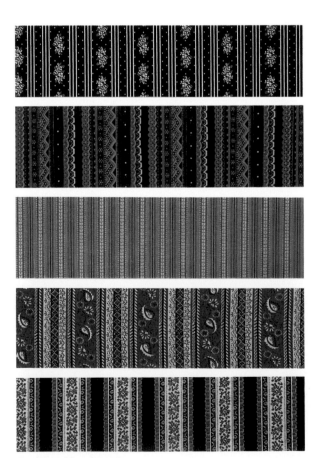

Traditional border stripes

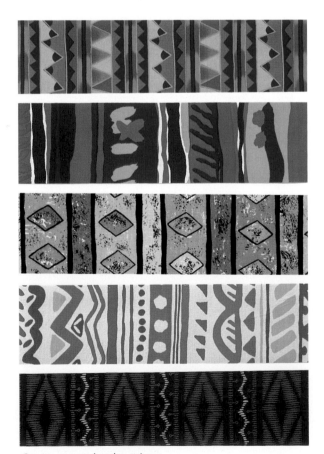

Contemporary border stripes

10

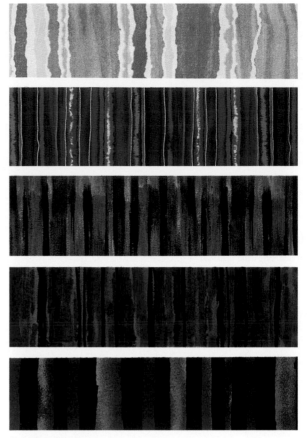

Marker-drawn stripes

Paintbrush stripes

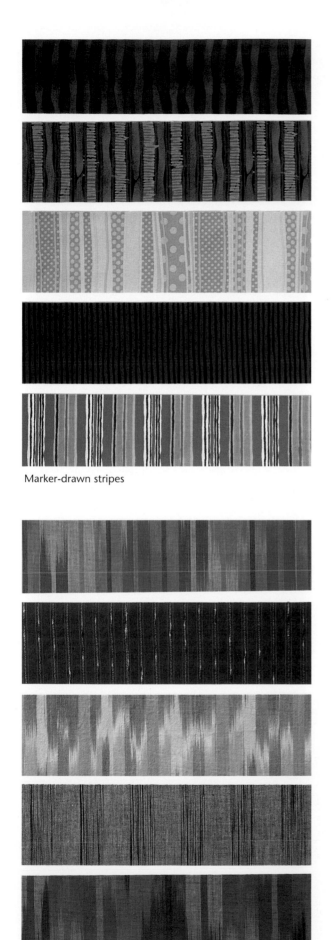

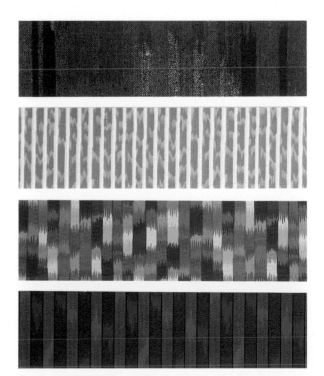

Woven ikat stripes

Printed (imitation) ikat stripes

Pattern Repeat

When a design is created for a fabric, it is made up of a specific unit, which is repeated over and over. The unit is called a pattern repeat. Some stripe patterns are simple and repeat themselves quickly, while other stripes run for a longer length. The stripes in decorator fabrics can have enormous repeats.

Determining the pattern repeat of a stripe can help you estimate how much yardage you need to buy. Small repeats are efficient because the stripe pattern is repeated often, and you won't need extra fabric. If you are only interested in one section of a large repeat, then you will need to buy more fabric. (Think creatively—you may be able to use the remaining sections in other parts of the project.)

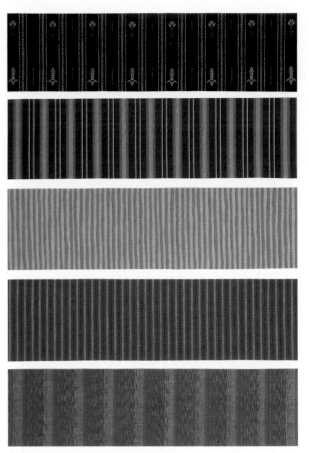

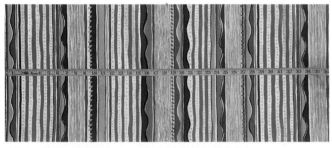

Measuring large pattern repeat in decorator fabric

Stripes with small pattern repeats

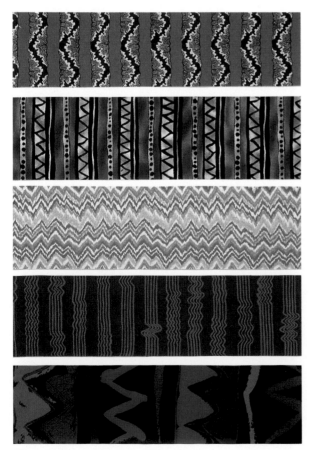

Zigzag stripes

Curved stripes

12

▦ *Expanding What Counts as a Stripe*

Don't be rigid when selecting stripes.

Unstraight Stripes

The lines don't have to be absolutely straight and parallel in stripe patterns. The overall effect is what is important.

Handmade Stripes

If you paint, air-brush, or tie-dye your fabrics, you can make your own stripes. (You can even use marbling to enhance ready-made stripes.) If you don't want to make the stripes yourself, you can buy these fabrics from fabric artists. Recently, fabric manufacturers have been reproducing the handmade "look."

Almost Stripes

Once you realize that stripes don't have to be literal stripe patterns to be stripes, you will look at printed fabrics in a different way.

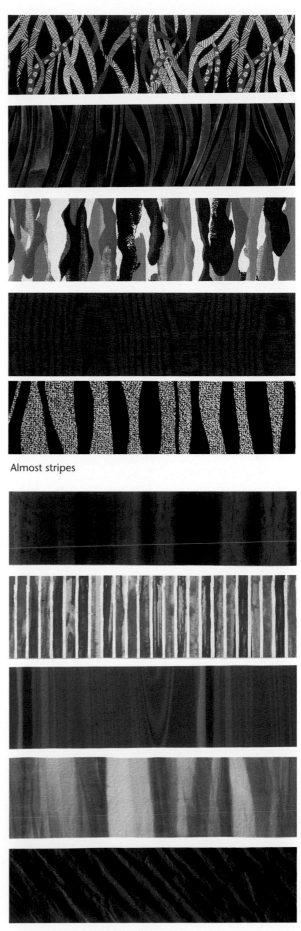

Almost stripes

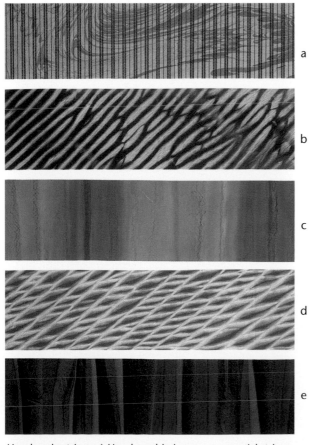

a
b
c
d
e

Handmade stripes a) Hand-marbled over commercial stripes by Ann Rhode; b) and e) Air-brushed fabrics from Lunn Fabrics; c) Hand-painted fabrics by Adrian Young; d) Shibori by Myhre

Commercial handmade stripes

Trapped stripes

Trapped Stripes

Striped portions are sometimes trapped in a patterned fabric that is not an all-over stripe. Although cutting only the trapped stripe is wasteful, you may find that you just need that little bit of stripe.

▤ *Mood*

In addition to having a physical structure and appearance, stripes can also be classified by mood. You can assess them according to their "feeling." I think about the feeling a fabric projects when I put theme fabrics together to create a story quilt[1]. I have now found that I can tell a story with stripes—it is just more abstract. If you look carefully, you can find clues to the story in the stripes I use.

If you look at the stripes pictured in this chapter, you will see that they can represent many moods, feelings, or themes. Comparing opposites is helpful. For example, can you find stripes that are somber or festive; prim-and-proper or flamboyant; or sweet-and-innocent or sophisticated?

Detail of *Firestorm II*, (78" x 78" quilt), Mary Mashuta, 1992

▤ *Why Don't Quilters Use More Stripes?*

Quilters often tell me that they can't find any stripes to buy, but I have discovered that they just have to learn to look for them. Stripes are available, but in most fabric stores the stripes are grouped with other fabric types, rather than displayed separately. A quilt shop owner once told me she didn't have many stripes in stock. In a quick five minute search of her store, I discovered 30 bolts! Because the stripes are mixed in with other fabrics, you have to make a conscious effort to see them.

My own search for stripes is a continual and constant process. I am always ready to see and buy stripes no matter what city, state, or country I am in. I have learned to look in other places fabrics are sold. Sometimes I even look in stores that sell decorator fabric (the fabric is more expensive, but it is also wider).

Some color combinations of stripes are easier to find. Two-color stripes such as black/white, red/white, and pink/white are abundant, but many multicolored stripes are available. You have to learn to look for them by broadening where you look, and what you are willing to buy. Use what you can find for a first project. Ask your quilt friends or guild members to search their stashes and trade fabrics with you.

Some quilters think there aren't any interesting stripes available. Fortunately, there are many wonderful woven and printed stripes being produced specifically for today's quilters. (Lines by Roberta Horton for Clothworks/Fasco, Nancy Crow for John Kaldor®, and the Jennifer Sampou and PilgrimRoy lines of fabrics for P&B Textiles are a few examples, but many other lines also include stripes.)

If you find that stripes are overwhelming or boring when you see them on the fabric bolt, try using a viewing window on the stripes. Simply cut a square or triangle the size of a quilt block pattern piece in the center of a plain piece of paper, and then view the stripes through the window opening. The window will make it easier for you to see how the stripe will look after it has been cut.

1. *Story Quilts: Telling Your Tale in Fabric by Mary Mashuta* (Lafayette, CA: C&T Publishing, 1992).

Using viewing window on striped fabric

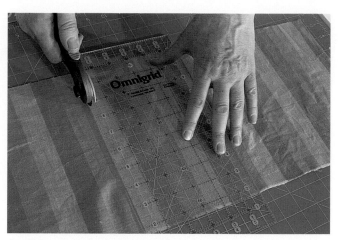

Parallel cutting of stripes with grided ruler

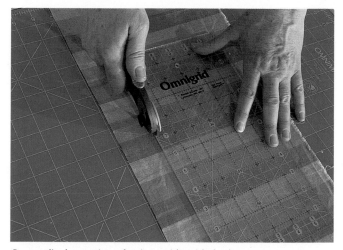

Perpendicular cutting of stripes with grided ruler

Bias cutting of stripes with grided ruler

Some quilters don't use stripes because they are afraid they can't cut them accurately. Actually, stripes are easy to cut using a rotary cutter and grided ruler because you can align the lines of the ruler with the lines of the stripe for parallel and perpendicular cuts. (I recommend Omnigrid® rulers because they have black and yellow lines printed on them. If the stripe colors don't show well against the black lines, they will show against the yellow. Some of their rulers also have diagonal lines for bias cuts.)

Before you cut, plan ahead so you can later stitch right beside or on top of a line. Cutting with a rotary cutter is an accurate way to cut stripes because you get a sharper edge, especially when you use a grided ruler or metal strip. Single layer cutting is the rule with stripes because you need to see what you are cutting. Spending more time on cutting accurately makes sewing the blocks together faster and easier. You can still stack cut the parts of your quilt that aren't stripes.

I have learned to buy stripes when I see them so they will be available when I want them. Often I am just buying fabric to add to my collection. A half yard is enough of most fabrics. If I run out, I can add something similar to the mix. Since striped fabric may look like Swiss cheese when I've cut my pattern pieces, it is better to start with larger pieces. If I like it and think it is really important, I may purchase from ¾ to 1½ yards. I may also consider just buying the half yard, and then purchasing several or all of the colorways. With a little effort over a period of time, you can build a nice stripe collection.

Chapter 2
Using Stripes in Quilts

Now that you have bought, begged, borrowed, bartered, or even made your own striped fabrics, you are ready to ask, "What happens next?" Delight in the fact that there are many uses for stripes in a quilt. Stripes can enhance the blocks, border, sashing, binding, and overall quilt design. While many blocks work well with stripes, some work better than others. It is exciting to see how an interesting striped fabric enlivens an otherwise ordinary block. Look for blocks and quilt designs that will benefit from the addition of striped fabrics. I'm always looking for "candidate" blocks, and have this in mind as I look through every new quilt book, magazine, or calendar that arrives at my house. Look through your own quilt reference library for candidate blocks. If your library isn't extensive, ask your quilt friends to let you review their materials. Also visit your local public library, or borrow materials from your quilting guild.

In addition to identifying candidate blocks, examine pictures of completed quilts and border designs. It's fun for me to imagine how I would incorporate stripes within a historical design; although, my quilts don't look historical once I've finished them. A wonderful source of inspiration and a good starting point are any of the books published in recent years by quilt research projects in many states.

As you "read" the pictures, forget about the fabrics used in the completed quilts. Ask yourself, "Where would I put stripes instead?" As an example of this process, notice how two of my quilts incorporate stripes in the same basic design. To create *Coming to Terms,* I used red and white stripes, and always placed the stripes in the same pieces and in the same position. When I made the second quilt, *Lessons Learned,* I made a conscious choice to put in as many stripes as possible.

2.1 *Coming to Terms,* 60¹/₂″ x 60¹/₂″, Mary Mashuta, 1990

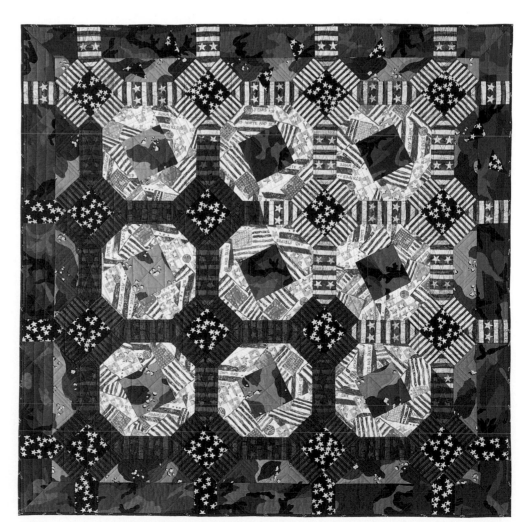

2.2 *Lessons Learned,* 60¹/₂″ x 60¹/₂″, Mary Mashuta, 1992

▤ *Finding Good Stripe Blocks*

There are lots of good stripe blocks around; but, just like finding good striped fabrics, you have to learn to look for them. Stripes can be used in many simple blocks (don't think the blocks have to be complex). Learning how to pick quilt blocks is an important first step to making a quilt with stripes, and understanding the difference between the positive and negative spaces in a quilt block is where you should start.

Understanding Positive and Negative Space

Although appliqué is not the focus of this book, positive and negative space is easier to understand in appliqué blocks since bits of fabric are sewn to a background square. Observe Kristina Becker's quilt, *Eight Birds and One Cat.* The birds, cat, leaves, and clever "vines" that join the blocks create the positive (the important) part of her design. The background fabric squares create the negative (or leftover) space. It just so happens the squares that Kristina used for her

background, or negative space, were cut from striped fabric rather than plain fabric. Note how she has made the quilt more playful by not always placing the striped squares in the same direction.

Many pieced blocks have positive and negative space. The positive part forms the design (such as a basket); the remaining, leftover space is the background or negative space. Together they make the block a complete unit. Just like completing a jigsaw puzzle, you have to fit all the pieces together before you are done.

When I was first selecting blocks for the book, I was most aware of what was happening in the positive space of each block. As time progressed, however, I was able to figure out how to use stripes in the negative space of some blocks. It takes more thought to use stripes in the negative space of pieced blocks because the fabric is cut up rather than used as a large piece (like it is for appliqué). Work toward placing stripes in the negative spaces of a block.

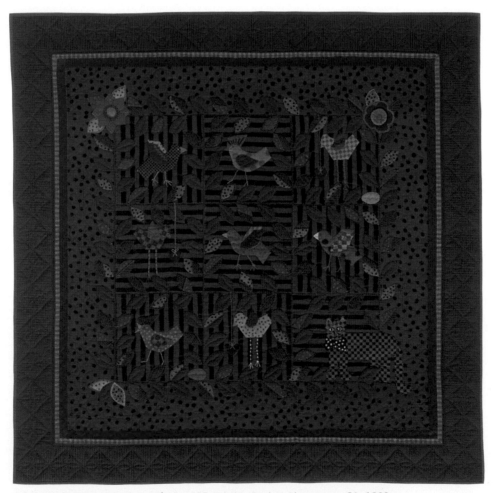

2.3 *Eight Birds and One Cat*, 52½" x 53", Kristina Becker, Pleasanton, CA, 1993; quilted by Ola Bonhager

18

Analyzing the Pieces in a Block

Stripes can make a block work for you. If the striped pieces connect with each other, they will engage your eye and lead it visually around the block. This is why I am naturally attracted to blocks that have a "hole" in the middle of the design. Stripes placed in the pieces around this hole form a larger visual unit, or segment, that you become aware of as your eye travels over the quilt. If the visual unit is repeated from block to block, the eye continues its trip around the surface of the quilt. The pieces around the hole are the positive space; the hole is the negative space. Pieces cut from stripes form chevrons at corners. These are called mitered corners, or Y seams.

The blocks I've selected use four main geometric shapes: squares, rectangles, triangles, and trapezoids (four-sided figures with two sides parallel). I routinely place stripes parallel, perpendicular, or diagonal to the edge of these shapes (a).

When rotary cutting stripes for a block, first plan a strategy to cut strips from the striped fabrics.

EXAMPLE

The Attic Window block needs two mirror-imaged trapezoids to form the mitered corner (2.4).

STRATEGY

Cut the strips, and then cut the trapezoids individually from each strip (2.5).

Note: Each piece is cut separately from the strip. The stripes are placed exactly alike so the pieces match = some waste of fabric.

SQUARES

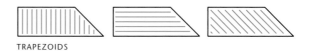

RECTANGLES

RIGHT-ANGLE TRIANGLES

ISOSCELES TRIANGLES

TRAPEZOIDS

a. Placing stripes in geometric shapes

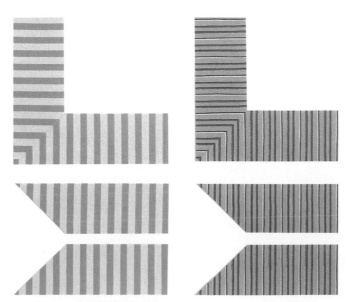

2.4 Even printed stripe (left) and uneven printed stripe (right)

2.5

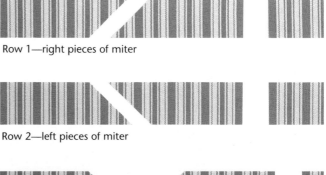

Row 1—right pieces of miter

Row 2—left pieces of miter

Row 3—left and right pieces cut in the same row

2.6 Even perpendicular stripe

2.7 Uneven parallel stripe

EXAMPLE

Cutting triangles from even, marker-drawn stripes. The lines are perpendicular to the hypotenuse[1] (2.6).

STRATEGY

The light pink stripe is selected as the center of each triangle.

Note: Very little waste occurs.

EXAMPLE

Cut triangles from uneven striped fabric. The lines are parallel to the hypotenuse. The strips may need to be wider to accommodate two sets of triangles (2.7).

STRATEGY

Group like triangles together when using uneven stripes (no one will notice that all the blocks aren't alike). For example: group like triangles together in the same border strip. You will end up with two sets of matching strips. Two corners will match, and two won't (few will notice unless the two sets are dramatically different).

Let's review some of the blocks I've selected.

POSSIBILITIES

Blocks with holes and mitered corners include the Attic Window, Beveled Window, and Mosaic Tile blocks (b–d).

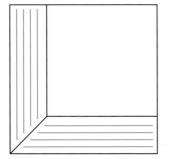

b. Attic Window block

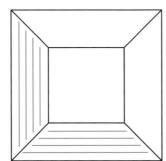

c. Beveled Window block

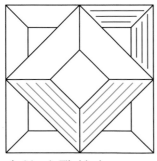

d. Mosaic Tile block

1. hypotenuse: the side opposite the right angle

POSSIBILITIES

Chevron corners are created in a Mitered Rectangle block and can be created in the two-triangle basket of a Quick Basket block (e,f).

e. Mitered Rectangle block   f. Quick Basket block

POSSIBILITIES

Rows of triangles pieced in stripes around a hole create concentric circles. An example is the Garden Path block (g).

Connections between Blocks

In addition to looking at larger visual units that can be created within a block, look at possibilities that can occur when blocks are joined to each other. Stripes can lead your eye from one block to the next, and create a new all-over design.

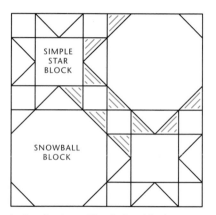

g. Garden Path block

POSSIBILITY

The triangles of a Simple Star block can connect with the corner triangles of a Snowball block to create a Star Lattice (h).

Pieces that form an X, or cross, trap the eye when they are pieced with stripes. The Xs in adjoining blocks connect with each other (visually, the Xs in alternating blocks also connect with each other) so when blocks made from stripes are pieced together an all-over grid is created.

POSSIBILITIES

Blocks with visual Xs include Nine Patch and Diagonal Cross, Cover Stripes, Interlocking X, and Picture X (i–l).

h. Star Lattice = Simple Star block + Snowball block

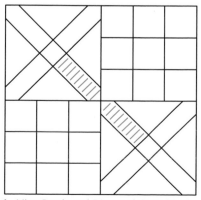

i. Nine Patch and Diagonal Cross blocks

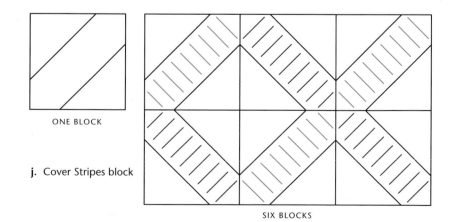

ONE BLOCK

j. Cover Stripes block

SIX BLOCKS

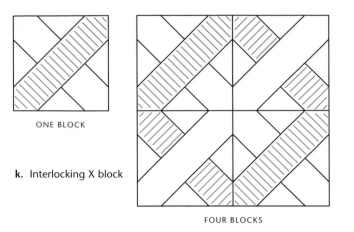

ONE BLOCK

k. Interlocking X block

FOUR BLOCKS

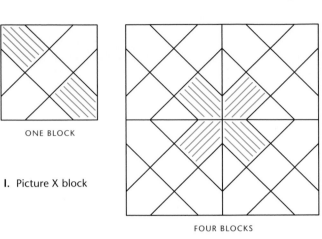

ONE BLOCK

l. Picture X block

FOUR BLOCKS

Grids

Continuous blocks pieced in stripes create all-over grids. They make it easy to work with positive and negative space.

Examples of all-over design are the Patriot's Quilt, Snake Trail, Parallelogram Zigag and Zigzag Miter blocks (m–p).

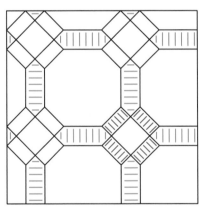

m. Patriot's Quilt block

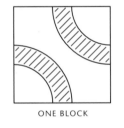

ONE BLOCK

n. Snake Trail block

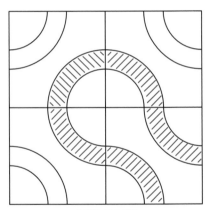

FOUR BLOCKS

ONE BLOCK

o. Parallelogram Zigzag block

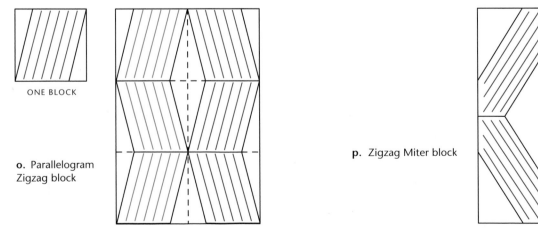

p. Zigzag Miter block

SIX BLOCKS

TWO BLOCKS

22

▤ *Playing with a Block*

Once I find a block, I play with varying the size of the block, the proportions of the block pieces, the position of the stripes in the pieces of the block, and the ways to combine like blocks in my final set. My play time is very important! You don't have to take the time to stitch your blocks, just look at the fabric through viewing windows (cut in plain paper) and make glued mock-ups. To make a glued mock-up, cut the pieces of the block without seam allowances and then glue them in place on the paper. (Place glue on the paper, not the fabric.)

Adapting the Block Size

When I made the Three-dimensional block, I made it in two sizes to compare how the stripes would appear once they were placed in the design. I also played with changing the orientation of the ikat stripe in the ice-cream cone shape. In hindsight, I could have also played with changing the position of the stripes in the other two pattern pieces.

POSSIBILITY

Change the size of the block; change the orientation of the stripes (2.8).

Blocks may look great by themselves, but we most often use them in repeated groups. I made four blocks so I could see how the blocks would relate to each other after they were set.

POSSIBILITY

Repeat four blocks to form adjoining blocks (2.9).

Making Alternating Blocks

When I played with the Garden Breeze block, I kept the block size consistent. I realized by reversing or mirror-imaging the block, I could create chevrons between blocks. (Adding two more pieces to my glued mock-ups was enough of a notation to remind me to reverse the blocks.)

POSSIBILITY

Reverse blocks = switch placement of two stripes in the positive and negative space (2.10).

10" BLOCK

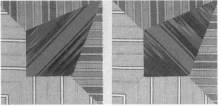

6" BLOCK

2.8 Three-dimensional block

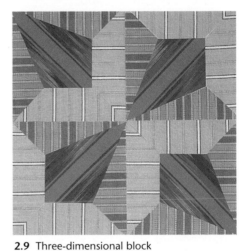

FOUR ADJOINING BLOCKS

2.9 Three-dimensional block

2.10 Garden Breeze block

BLOCKS REVERSED

STRIPES SWITCHED IN POSITIVE AND NEGATIVE SPACE

Adapting the Block Proportions

As a quilt artist, I can also change the proportions within a particular block to better suit me and the stripes I am using. Although the size of the stripes can't be changed, the size of the individual pieces can be changed.

POSSIBILITY

Make the center square in the Garden Breeze block larger or smaller to increase or decrease the amount of positive and negative space (2.11).

Adapting Blocks to Make Them More Complicated

In your search for quilt blocks, you might skip some blocks because they contain too many pieces. Remember, as an artist, you decide how big a block should be. Blocks with many pieces can always be made larger so the pieces are bigger.

POSSIBILITY

Four 14" Garden Path blocks (2.12)

2.11 Garden Breeze block

LARGER CENTER SQUARE   SMALLER CENTER SQUARE

Making the Garden Path block larger made it possible for me to break it down further so I could show off my stripes in a more complicated way.

POSSIBILITY

Four 24" Garden Path blocks = divided trapezoids into triangles + pieced gift box in center hole (2.13).

2.12 *Corey's Quilt,* 35½" x 36", Mary Mashuta, 1992; in the collection of Corey Sloan Sisney

2.13 *Christmas Boxes,* 47" x 47", Mary Mashuta, 1993; quilted by Rhondi Hindman

■ *Overcoming Problems with Stripes*

Learn to look at problems as challenging, rather than negative, events when you work with stripes. Learn to play and come up with creative solutions.

What to Do if the Stripes Are Boring

If you're working on your striped quilt, and it starts to become boring (only in the design, of course!), learn to increase the "activity level" of the project. You'll find that any, several, or all of the following solutions will work.

SOLUTIONS:

- My sister, Roberta Horton, would say to cut the stripes "casually off-grain."

- My sister would also tell you to make your blocks "less perfect" and "more spontaneous" (2.14).

- Add stripes with more colors.

- Add one or more colorways of the same stripe.

- Add a wider variety of stripe types.

- Add other types of fabric including wild prints, plaids, wispy solids, and/or hand-dyed fabrics.

- Make the quilting design more complex.

- Add more colors of quilting thread.

- Add thick, meandering perle cotton or sashiko thread if hand quilting.

- Add machine embroidery.

- Add embellishments such as buttons, beads, hanging threads, and appliquéd triangles.

- Add a lively border.

- Place quilt in an askew, or tilted set

- Add bias binding.

Try a combination of additives like I did for *Night Noises: Londolozi.*

SOLUTION

Add a variety of stripes or other print types, and machine embroidery, beads, and hanging threads (2.15).

2.14 An antique block that is "less perfect" and "more spontaneous"

2.15 Detail of *Night Noises: Londolozi*, Mary Mashuta (quilt shown on page 42)

2.16 Jewel Box block (too spotty)

2.17 Jewel Box block (calmer striped substitute)

What to Do if the Stripes Are Too Spotty

Prints with lots of small motifs, and/or strong value or color contrast between the motifs and the background can be "spotty." The spots make your eye jump around the design in an agitated way. Striped fabric can be spotty, too. For my *Hearts Quilt,* I began with a spotty, medium-sized heart, striped fabric. Then, I added two colorways of a smaller-scale heart striped fabric, which I planned to criss-cross within the blocks.

PROBLEM

Spotty red-white-and-blue stripes (2.16)

SOLUTION:

Substitute a calmer stripe for red-white-and-blue colorway of small stripe (2.17).

What to Do if Colors Optically Bleed

Previously, I discussed how quilt blocks have positive and negative space (page 18). To clearly "read" the blocks, you need to see the two parts as separate. Yet, sometimes what I've planned for one part accidentally bleeds, or blends, into the other part. This is great for art quilts which often rely on special effects; however, bleeding may be an upsetting event in more traditional quilts.

PROBLEM

Pink color in stripe bleeds into negative space pink print (2.18).

SOLUTION

Be more careful in cutting squares; place contrasting colors at edge of squares (2.19).

2.18 Attic Window block (stripe bleeds)

2.19 Attic Window (more carefully cut stripes)

What to Do if You Run Out of Fabric?

One of the biggest problems you may encounter, when making a quilt with striped fabric, is running out of your stripe. It is unnerving, but I know my quilts always end up more interesting if I run out of a fabric. Long ago I learned to substitute similar fabrics when I ran out of a print or solid. If you are daring, you can do the same substitutions with stripes.

PROBLEM

Not enough of one stripe to make four complete blocks (2.20)

SOLUTION

Substitute similar stripe in fourth block (2.21).

If you have purchased other colorways of the stripe, you may be able to substitute them in the design. This worked successfully for me in my *Coming to Terms* quilt (page 17) and *Memories of Christmas Past* (page 28).

2.20 Christmas Box block (one stripe only)

2.21 Christmas Box block (substituted stripe)

▤ *Deciding on a Project*

There are many blocks and project ideas presented in this book. Once you find a block you like, you can then decide how much time you want to invest in a project. Choices vary from the quick and easy to the longer and more challenging. For example, start with my Tourist Shirt block. I've included the illustration, which is an 8″ block, in order for you to create a 16″ block of your own. Enlarge the illustration to form a 16″ square, and then divide the block into separate pieces as shown. Make the templates for the 16″ block by adding a ¼″ seam allowance to each piece.

Begin at the level of using stripes where you are the most comfortable. One stripe may be enough for a first, simple project. Or, you can put together a striped fabric collection for a more artful quilt.

PROBLEM

Little quilting time

SOLUTION

Small wallhanging = single block + pieced striped border (2.22)

2.22 *Christmas Shirt,* 24″ x 24″, Mary Mashuta, 1994; in the collection of Ann Merrel and Judy Martin

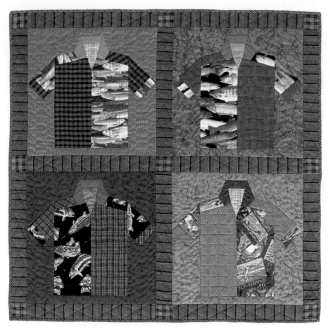

2.23 *Gone Fishin'*, 37¹/₂" x 37¹/₂", Karen Dugas, Pleasant Hill, 1995; quilted by Karen Dugas and Becky Keck

2.24 *Memories of Christmas Past*, 44" x 44", Mary Mashuta, 1991

If you have more time and the inclination, make more blocks!

POSSIBILITY

Multiple blocks + simple sashing and border (2.23)

POSSIBILITY

Multiple blocks + pieced sashing and border (2.24)

POSSIBILITY

Multiple blocks in free-form set + pieced border + an askew set (2.25)

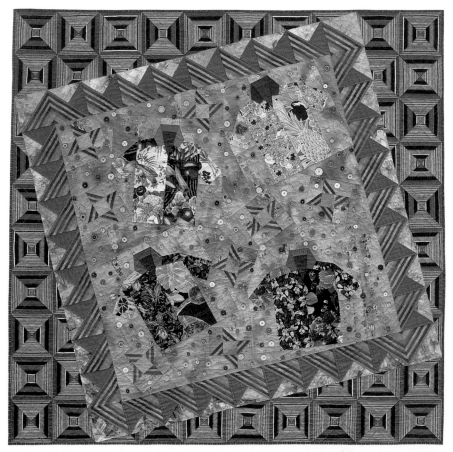

2.25 *Tourist in the Gourmet Ghetto*, 59¹/₂" x 59¹/₂", Mary Mashuta, 1994

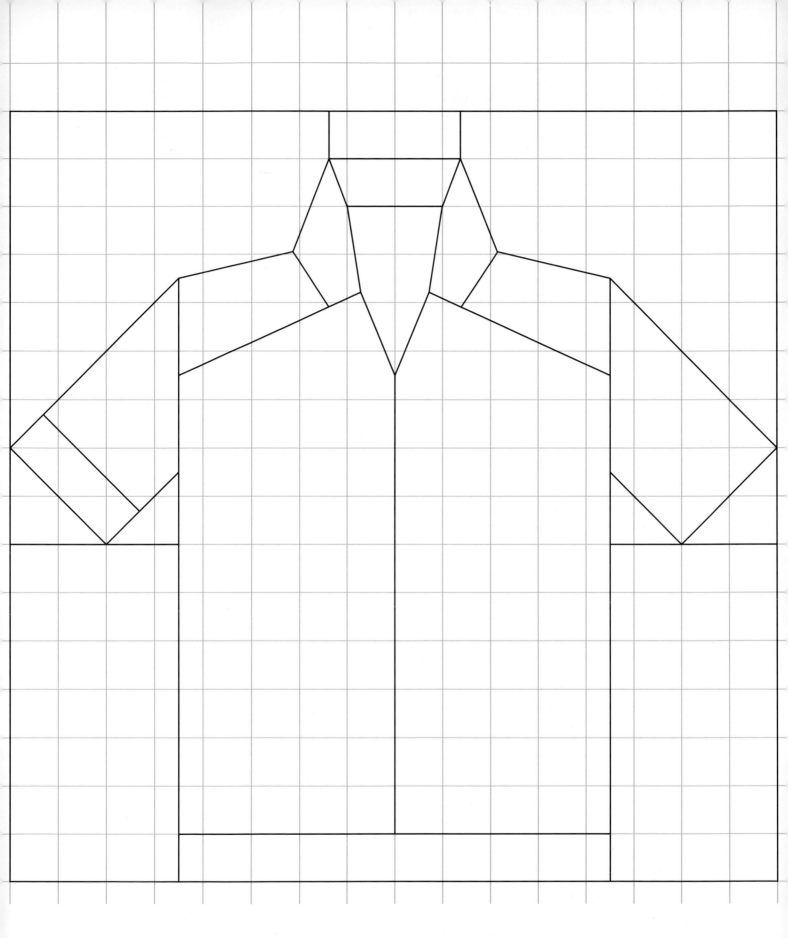

The quilts in this book featuring the Tourist Shirt block are all based on a 16" block. The pattern above is for an 8" block.

Chapter 3

Attic Windows and Stripes

P lay is not just the "work" of children. Thoughts progress into other thoughts, letting your mind discover new solutions. As a quilter, you can discover a lot about stripes by playing with Attic Windows.

The Attic Window block is one of the simplest quilt blocks: trapezoid pieces form a two-sided frame around a square window. The frame pieces join in a mitered corner. Traditionally, the frame has one light

piece and one dark. The square window is often cut from a conversation print. (The term conversation print simply means that the design has a specific theme. The motifs are recognizable objects such as pumpkins, sewing machines, or cars—I guess that some may become so thrilled with the motifs, they have to have conversations about them.)

SEWING THE MITER IN AN ATTIC WINDOW BLOCK

Step 1. With right sides facing and using a ¼″ seam allowance, sew Piece 1 and Piece 2 together. Stop at the red dot and backstitch ¼″ from the edge (shown by the dot in the illustration).

Step 2. Repeat Step 1 to sew Piece 1 and Piece 3 together.

Step 3. Sew the diagonal edge of Piece 2 and Piece 3 together. Stop at the red dot and backstitch ¼″ from the edge (shown by the dot in the illustration).

TIPS

Leave the pins in while you sew to help keep the pieces from distorting. Fingerpress the seams after each step, and then press the seams with an iron after all the seams are sewn.

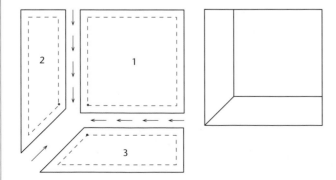

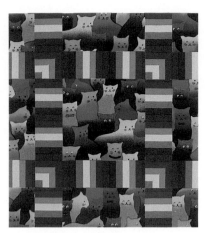

3.1 Everything runs together

3.2 *Cat Windows,* 35" x 35", Mary Mashuta, 1994; unquilted, pieced top

Let's see what happens when I experiment with an Attic Window block. First, I'll place stripes in the frame pieces (usually I place the stripes perpendicular to the long edge so they show off better). See how I carefully picked a rainbow stripe to go with my rainbow conversation print—but what a miscalculation!

PROBLEM

When the blocks are set side by side, everything runs together = it all becomes mush (3.1)!

SOLUTION

A two-colored stripe makes it possible to distinguish the frames and the windows (3.2).

PROBLEM

One-stripe frames + repeated print windows = safe and boring (3.3)

SOLUTION

Two-stripe frames + repeated print windows = more interesting (3.4)

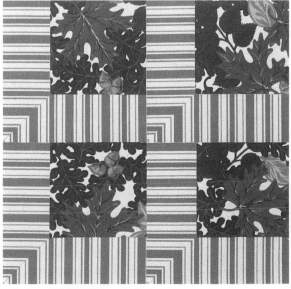

3.3 Safe, yet boring

3.4 More interesting

3.5 Bleeding colors

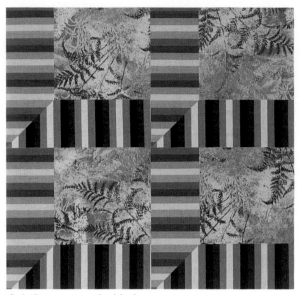

3.6 Can now see the block

PROBLEM

Two-colorway one-stripe frames + low contrast, same print windows = bleeding of colors (3.5)

SOLUTION

Two-colorway one-stripe frames + higher contrast repeated print windows = possible to see pieces in block (3.6)

Once you are able to distinguish the parts of the block, and place your stripes and prints effectively, the fun begins. Observe the following block variations.

POSSIBILITY

Assorted multistripe scrap frames + same print windows (3.7)

POSSIBILITY

Two-stripe frames + assorted scrap plaids and stripes windows (fabric samples from Japan) (3.8)

3.7 Assorted multistripe frames

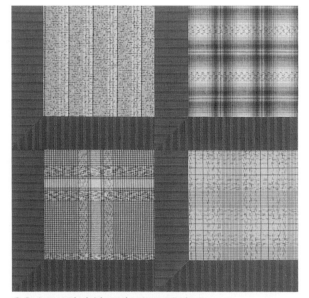

3.8 Assorted plaids and stripes windows

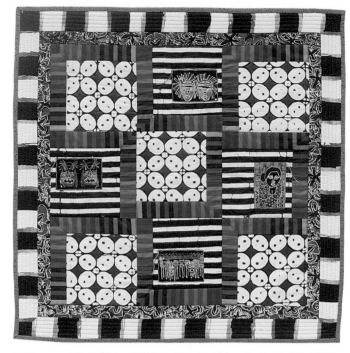

3.10 *Dinosaur Windows*, 36" x 36", Mary Mashuta, 1995; quilted by Mary Mashuta and Tracy Allen

3.11 *a⌣pa.ini?*, 36½" x 37", Joan Capron Helm, Portland, OR, 1992

If you can play with the block, you can also play with the way it is set. Both Joan Helm and I decided to play with a flip flop set, yet our quilts couldn't have been more different. I wanted to show off a collection of dinosaur fabrics, and Joan wanted to incorporate postcard size Indonesian batik pictures.

(a⌣pa.ini?, means What's happening?)

POSSIBILITY

One-stripe frames + same print windows + flip flop set (3.10)

POSSIBILITY

One-stripe frames + one-stripe windows (with batik prints) + flip flop set (3.11)

Quilters set other blocks on point, so why not Attic Windows?

POSSIBILITY

Scrap stripe frames + same print windows + flip flop set + blocks set on point (3.12)

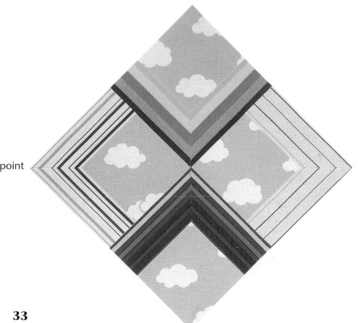

3.12 Flip flop blocks set on point

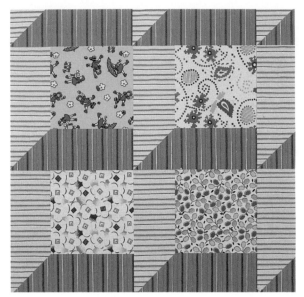

3.13 Cottage Window design

3.14 Appliqué hearts

PROBLEM

When Attic Windows are sewn together, you end up with two optically heavy sides formed by the frame pieces from each block.

The Cottage Window design solves this problem. Along two edges of the quilt, additional frames are added to the two optically lighter sides (formed by the windows). Now all of the edges of the quilt have equal visual weight.

SOLUTION

Cottage Window design. Two-colorway stripe frames + assorted reproduction 1930s print windows (3.13)

If you like to appliqué, you can embellish your Attic Windows with cut-outs.

POSSIBILITY

Two-color stripe frames + one print window + scrap appliqué hearts (3.14)

Now let's see what happens when we play some more with the window part of the Attic Window block. Compare the following pairs of blocks where I have divided the window into triangles. Note that it makes a difference whether I cut my stripe parallel or perpendicular to the hypotenuse of the triangle.

BLOCK

Two-colorway decorator stripe frame + a leaf print window (3.15)

VARIATION

Four-triangle window = stripe (cut parallel) + print; triangles opposing (3.16)

3.15 Decorator stripe with leaf print

3.16 Four-triangle window variation

BLOCK

Two-border stripe frames (cut perpendicular) + four-triangle window = Bull's Eye Window (cut parallel) (3.19)

VARIATION

Two-border stripe frames (cut parallel) + four-triangle window = cross (cut perpendicular) (3.20)

So far I've played with one block at a time. But, the Bull's Eye and Cross Window variations shown would be interesting if they were alternated in a quilt. Let's look at some other possibilities. I have placed some stripes in adjoining, rather than opposing, triangles.

FOUR REPEAT BLOCKS

Two homespun stripe frames + four-triangle window = adjoining triangles dark/light (3.21)

VARIATION

Straight Furrows Log Cabin set (3.22)

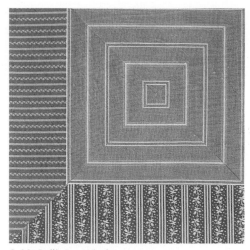

3.19 Bull's Eye Window variation

3.20 Cross Window variation

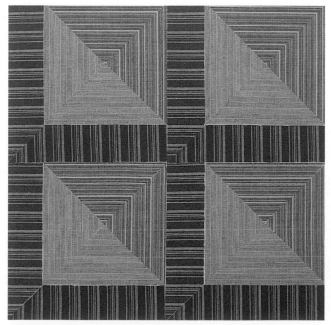

3.21 Half dark, half light window

3.22 Straight Furrows set

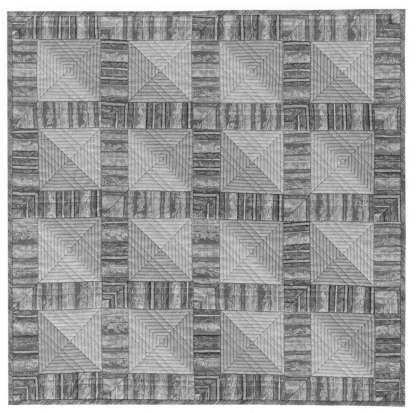

3.23 *Green and Orange Stripes,* 36" x 36", Mary Mashuta, 1995

By playing with the blocks on the previous page, I discovered that I could rotate alternate windows and create a connecting secondary pattern in the windows of adjoining blocks. The frames are bold; the diagonal color slant is subtle. Here I have used completely different stripes in this small quilt.

POSSIBILITY

Two-colorway, marker-drawn stripe frames + two-colorway stripe window = set in Straight Furrows variation (3.23)

Finally, I experimented by using Nine Patch windows in Attic Windows.

PROBLEM

Stripes too static (3.24)

SOLUTION

Randomly rotate one square to make it "less perfect" (3.25).

3.24 Too static

3.25 Rotate one square

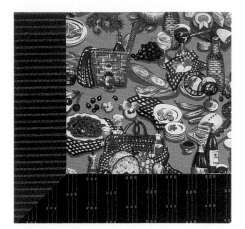

3.28 Spotty print

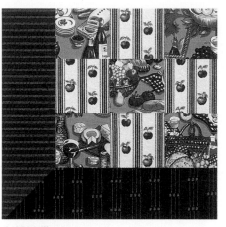

3.29 Still spotty

3.30 Substitute homespun stripe

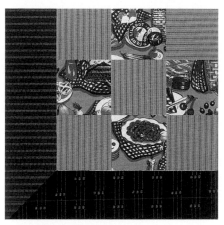

3.31 Subtler homespun stripe

PROBLEM

Spotty print used in window (3.28)

NINE PATCH WINDOW #1 SOLUTION

Add border stripe = still too spotty (3.29)

NINE PATCH WINDOW #2 SOLUTION

Substitute homespun stripe (3.30)

NINE PATCH WINDOW #3 SOLUTION

Add a subtler homespun stripe (3.31)

NINE PATCH WINDOW #4 SOLUTION

Use both homespuns = forget about spotty print and spotty border stripe (3.32)

3.32 Use homespun stripes

Now that you have formed a base understanding of the way stripes act in one quilt block, you're ready to explore some other blocks.

Chapter 4

Beveled Windows and Stripes

Y ou may think of Beveled Window, a block of my own naming, as the Spools block because the pattern pieces are the same. In both blocks, four frame pieces join in four mitered corners. There is always a center square, window, or hole. Of course, this block also has much in common with the Attic Window block.

The frame of the Beveled Window block forms the positive space, while the hole in the center is the negative space. Since there is always positive space at the block's edge, you need to consider what happens when stripes are placed in the frame. If a stripe frame block is alternated with a print frame block, you don't have to worry about stripes touching stripes. However, print selection is important. Observe what happens when I try an alternating stripe/print block arrangement in two similar pieces—I get quite different results.

▤ *Alternating Stripe and Print Blocks*

The quilt *North Country* looks like it could go in a log cabin in the backwoods. Even though I was working toward a homespun feeling, I used a contemporary marker-drawn stripe that pulled the myriad of colors together.

POSSIBILITY

Marker-drawn stripe frames + homespun check frames = alternating blocks with same print windows (4.1)

PROBLEM

Alternating marker-drawn border stripe and print frames + same print windows = spotty (4.2)

In the second example, I went from a 10″ block to a 12″ block and used nine rather than four blocks. The quilt top was a lesson in using spotty, or busy prints. The visual activity level escalated sharply. Everything jumps around because the bright colors used in the stripe and heart patterns contrast sharply against the dark blue background. (The design contrast is lessened in the window print with a pale blue background.) Can you think of a solution, short of not finishing the top?

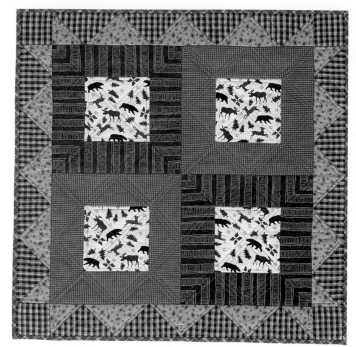

4.1 *North Country*, 25" x 25", Mary Mashuta, 1995

4.2 *Nursery Time*, 42" x 42", Mary Mashuta, 1994. Unquilted top

▤ *Combining Striped Blocks*

When Beveled Window blocks are pieced in assorted
stripes and set next to each other in a scrap effect,
each block will read as a separate unit. However, if you
choose to use only one stripe, take the time to think
what will happen when the blocks touch. If all of the
blocks are exactly alike, they will mush together and
become difficult to read as individual units.

One-Colorway Blocks

Changing the orientation of the stripes that are cut
for the frames lets the viewer know when one block
ends and another begins.

POSSIBILITY

One-colorway stripe blocks = one perpendicular cut
stripe with one parallel cut stripe = easy to see and sew
(4.3)

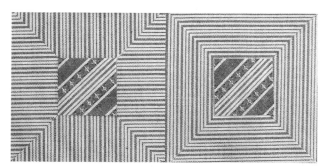

4.3 Easy to see and sew

Two-Colorway Blocks

If the blocks are pieced from different colorways of the same stripe, you will know where blocks begin and end because of the color change.

POSSIBILITY

Two-colorway stripe blocks = one perpendicular cut stripe + one parallel cut stripe = easy to see and sew (4.4)

POSSIBILITY

Two-colorway stripe blocks = both parallel cut = easy to see, but hard to sew (4.5)

Two colorways can be used effectively to create transparency if you use a perpendicular rather than a parallel cut. When the lines join those in the next block, the eye just keeps going. Secondary patterns also occur when the mitered corners meet. (Accuracy in matching the stripes is, of course, very important.)

POSSIBILITY

Two-colorway stripe blocks = both perpendicular cut = easy to see and moderately difficult to sew (4.6)

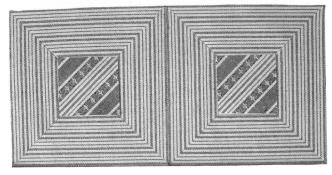

4.4 Easy to see and sew

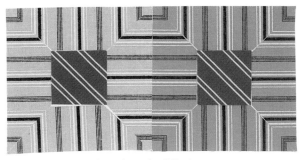

4.5 Easy to see, hard to sew

4.6 Easy to see and moderately difficult to sew

SEWING TWO PARALLEL CUT STRIPE BLOCKS TOGETHER

A. Cut so the ¼" seam allowance ends at the side of the line;

B. Pin parallel, rather than perpendicular;

C. Pin through the stitching line;

D. Keep the pins in until you are ready to stitch, then remove them slowly as you sew forward

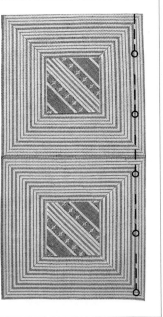

SEWING TWO PERPENDICULAR CUT BLOCKS TOGETHER

A. Match the stripes on the blocks to be sewn;

B. Pin the ends (or seam lines);

C. Pin the middle;

D. For larger blocks, add additional pins as necessary;

E. Place pin heads away from edge. Leave the pins in while you stitch (simply sew over them)

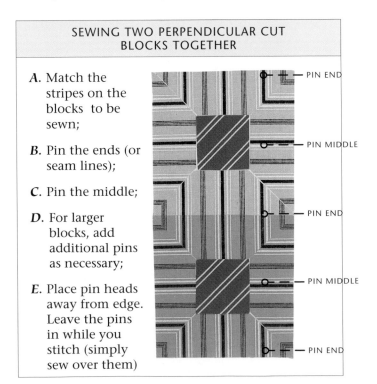

PIN END

PIN MIDDLE

PIN END

PIN MIDDLE

PIN END

Taking Advantage of Special Stripes

Occasionally, stripe patterns lend themselves to special effects. Take the time to really look at your stripes to decide if they have unique qualities. Here a more complex stripe had a consistent pattern of lines clustering in an alternating light/dark pattern. I knew the shadowing would add dimension when the blocks were joined, but I had no idea I would get an optical pinwheel at the junction of four blocks!

POSSIBILITY

One-colorway stripe blocks = both perpendicular cut, alternating light/dark center placement (4.8)

I used these blocks in *Pete Bowls a 259* to help fill leftover space. Note that you also can tell where the larger polychromatic stripe blocks begin and end because I changed the diagonal direction of the alternating blocks.

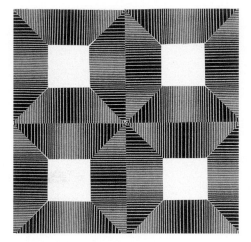

4.8 Blocks become dimensional

POSSIBILITY

Small one-color stripe blocks in alternating light/dark placement + large, multicolor Marimekko® diagonally cut stripe blocks in opposing placement (4.9)

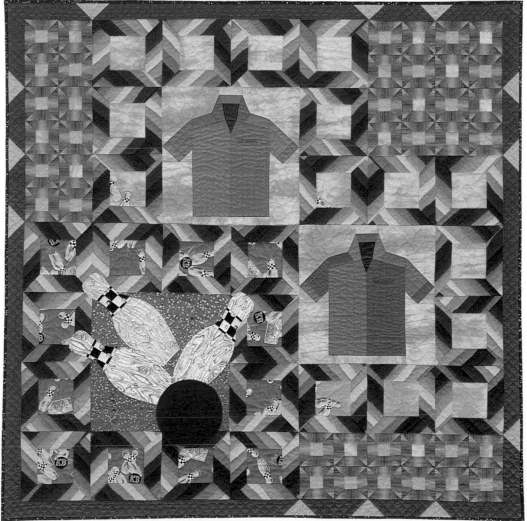

4.9 *Pete Bowls a 259*, 57" x 58", Mary Mashuta, 1992

41

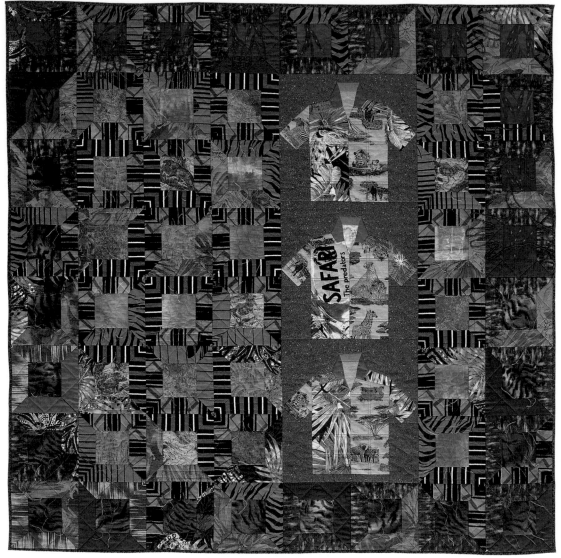

4.10 *Night Noises: Londolozi*, 62" x 62", Mary Mashuta, 1991

Two-Stripe Blocks

It is possible to make the Beveled Window block less rigid by using two stripes, rather than one, in each block. I had a half yard of one dirty green, black, and white stripe when I wanted to make a quilt in antici-pation of a trip to South Africa. I looked through my fabric collection and pulled out anything that would blend "colorwise" and could pass as a stripe when cut. I found one marker-drawn stripe, one ikat stripe, one animal print, and several Japanese Yukata prints that could be selectively cut.

POSSIBILITY

Two-fabric frames, many using one or two stripes + assorted print windows (4.10)

Three-Stripe Blocks

You may have noticed that stripes can also be added to the window of the Beveled Window block (see examples on pages 39–40 [4.3-4.6]). Using diagonally cut squares from one stripe and arranging them in the same orientation makes for a consistent negative space, which ties the quilt together. Jane Samuelson selected a small-scale stripe for her windows. Her quilt moves from light to dark in vertical rows. Blocks are consistent within rows, but there is sometimes varia-tion from block to block because of ikat weaving.

POSSIBILITY

Two-fabric frames in rows + one-stripe windows (4.11)

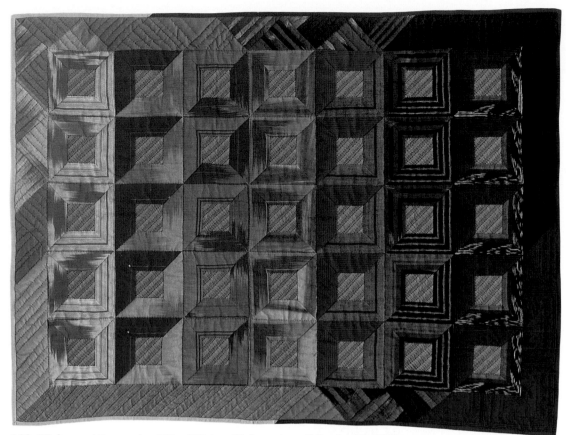

4.11 *Wisdom and Compassion,* 39" x 29", Jane W. Samuelson, El Cerrito, CA, 1993

Changing the Set

Beveled Window blocks can be arranged in a more complex manner similar to those in *Night Noises: Londolozi* or *Pete Bowls a 259.* It is also possible to set the block on point. Christine Davis created two sets of blocks for *Victoriana.* She cut up a large scale border stripe to frame a black and white Victorian print of young girls. (Because of the parallel cut, scale, and busyness of the stripe, the frames no longer read as stripes.) Then, she filled in the background blocks with a small-scale black and white stripe paired with a small-scale print. This combination doesn't have the same visual impact as the first set of blocks, so they don't fight for attention. These blocks work well as a negative space filler.

POSSIBILITY

Alternate sets of Beveled Window blocks = set on point (4.12)

4.12 *Victoriana,* 35" x 35", Christine Davis, Redmond, WA, 1993

43

≣ *Beveled Window Block Variations*

The window portion of the Beveled Window block can be divided like the windows of the Attic Window block. I guess you could call the following versions fractured windows.

Four-Triangle Beveled Window Blocks

POSSIBILITY

Two-colorway, ikat stripe frames + two-colorway, four-triangle Bull's Eye Window blocks (4.13)

   It is also possible to change the proportions within the block. The second set of blocks appears livelier because I mixed the colorways in the windows.

POSSIBILITY

Two-colorway ikat stripe frames + two-colorway mixed Bull's Eye Window blocks = changed block proportions (4.14)

4.13 Two-colorway blocks   **4.14** Mixed colorways, changed proportions

Three-Triangle Beveled Window Blocks

POSSIBILITY

Two-colorway frame + three-triangle stripe window = standard set (4.15)

POSSIBILITY

 Two-colorway frame with three-triangle stripe window = flip flop set (4.16)

Positive/Negative Three-Triangle Beveled Window Blocks

Four blocks of the three-triangle Beveled Window blocks work nicely as a larger unit when you work with a positive/negative format of two stripes.

4.15 Standard set

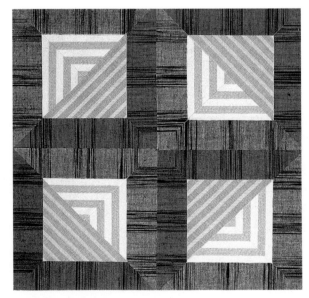

4.16 Flip flop set

POSSIBILITY

Two-stripe frame with three-triangle window (two-triangle stripe with conversation print triangle) = rotating set (4.17)

By adding sashing to the four-square units, you have started a quilt. For years, I've collected fabric to make a middle-of-the-night New York City Checker Cab quilt. In addition to collecting yellow fabrics, black-and-white checkerboards, and nighttime stars fabrics, I collected stripes. I sought anything between black-and-white and gray-and-white stripes.

POSSIBILITY

Eighteen stripes organized into nine three-triangle, positive/negative Beveled Window units + sashing (4.18)

4.17 Rotating positive/negative set

4.18 *Checker Cab: New York City, 2:00 A.M.*, 46$\frac{1}{2}$" x 46$\frac{1}{2}$" work-in-progress, Mary Mashuta

4.19 It never ends

4.20 Self-contained

Two-Frame, Four-Triangle Beveled Window Blocks

The basic Beveled Window block can be divided yet another way. When you erase two frames, the segments turn into large triangles and you get a two-frame, four-triangle Beveled Window. The stripe orientation changes the appearance of the block. The stripes can make the blocks look never-ending or self-contained. My first blocks were a real surprise.

The block adapts well to three stripes, but experiment with the orientation of the stripes.

PROBLEM

Large triangles have perpendicular (to the hypotenuse) stripes = never ending (4.19)

SOLUTION

Change large triangles to parallel (to the hypotenuse) stripes = self-contained (4.20).

POSSIBILITY

1960s border stripe + 1960s and contemporary prints + printed ikat stripe = nostalgia (4.21)

POSSIBILITY

Woven and printed stripes + homespun checks = country look (4.22)

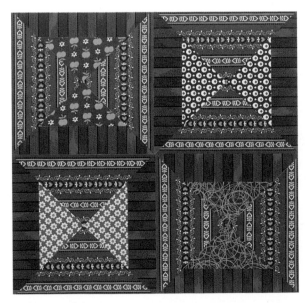

4.21 Nostalgia

4.22 Country Look

Abstracted Beveled Window Block

I decided to make abstracted blocks as a final statement for my Beveled Window adventures. This is where my journey led me: *Yulara: Journey to the Red Center* is based on a visit and a photo essay of Yulara, a tourist accommodations center, at Uluru (formally Ayres Rock), Australia. I collected fabrics for the quilt for two years. My collection contained Aboriginal prints; American prints; hand-dyed, tie-dyed, and air-brushed fabrics; a vintage 1880 woven stripe; and 1990s printed stripes. Quite a mix! When I got ready to make the quilt, I gathered my collection of fabrics, looked at my slides again, and began piecing abstracted Beveled Window blocks. I decided the blocks could contain two or three frames, but never four.

POSSIBILITY

Assorted, abstracted Beveled Window blocks (4.23)

4.23 *Yulara: Journey to the Red Center*, 70" x 78", Mary Mashuta, 1993

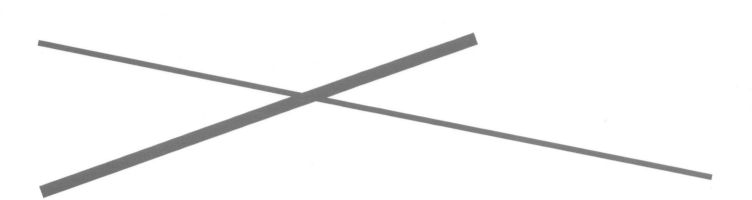

Chapter 5

Using Positive and Negative Space

*J*ust as positive and negative space in blocks helps you to read the pattern, blocks with a strong, clearly defined difference between positive and negative space can enhance a presentation of stripes.

▤ Mosaic Tile Block

One of my all-time favorite blocks is Mosaic Tile. It's a more complicated block than the Beveled Window because it has additional pieces added to the central window and frame. However, they are just more windows and frames. If you are selecting stripes for both sets of frames, consider the second set the secondary positive space.

There are four sets of positions for stripes in the Mosaic Tile block.

Mosaic Tile block stripe positions

Remember that you can change the size of the block, as well as the proportions of individual pieces, to better showcase your stripes. If a stripe is placed perpendicular to the frame edges, there are few problems if the stripe is even. Just check to make sure you have good corners. Shift a viewing window across your stripe to determine which lines you want at the center and which lines you want in the miters. If a choice is necessary, consider the corners before the middle.

Placing the stripe parallel to the edge in either of the sets of frames may present problems, particularly when the stripe scale is large. Make sure you see enough of the stripe to know it is a stripe. Remember, if you are only using one stripe, you can adjust the frame proportions to get a good stopping place between two lines. It won't make that much difference if the square or triangles are a little bigger or a little smaller. If you're using an assortment of stripes for your set of blocks, you don't have the luxury of making changes—you have to select a block size and then make the stripes fit in as best you can.

PROBLEM

Parallel inner stripe doesn't have a good stopping place = slightly larger window would have been ideal (5.1)

The Mosaic Tile block looks great drawn large, and it can give you an opportunity to display a piece of decorator chintz with some larger scale decorator stripes.

POSSIBILITY

24" Mosaic Tile block wallhanging = two stripes + decorator print (5.2)

5.1 Poor stripe placement in center

5.2 *Bouquet Mosaic*, 24" x 24", Mary Mashuta, 1995; quilted by Mary Mashuta and Ann Rhode

A smaller Mosaic Tile block is a nice size for a small baby quilt or "gift for baby" wallhanging. Find a baby border stripe for the large frame and a complementing, less-important stripe for the corner frames. Adjoining blocks can be distinguished because you change the direction of your stripe in the corner frames.

POSSIBILITY

10" Mosaic Tile blocks = border stripe + minor stripe + wispy print (5.3)

If you're lucky enough to find four colorways of a pastel stripe, try a more adventuresome baby quilt. To keep the sewing uncomplicated, I changed the stripe direction in the adjoining blocks.

POSSIBILITY

16" Mosaic Tile blocks = four-colorway stripe + larger stripe + baby prints (5.4)

5.3 Detail of *Teddy Bear Mosaic*, (30" x 30" quilt), Mary Mashuta, 1995

5.4 *Animal Parade*, 44" x 44", Mary Mashuta, 1995

50

If you're ready to try an art quilt, individually compose your blocks on a design wall. I tried to see how many stripes I could include in my second quilt, *Firestorm II,* which commemorated a disastrous fire in the Oakland/Berkeley hills. I looked for prints and stripes that portrayed windy sky and flames.

POSSIBILITY

Individually composed 16" Mosaic Tile blocks = theme stripes and prints (5.5)

Removing one quadrant and interlocking the three remaining sections in a series of blocks makes the Mosaic Tile block more abstract. I put together two sets of stripes. Nine stripes from South Africa were used for the positive spaces; seven colorways of an alternating light/dark stripe were used in the negative spaces.

POSSIBILITY

Individually composed, interlocked, and abstracted Mosaic Tile blocks = set of major stripes + set of minor stripes (5.6)

5.5 Detail of *Firestorm II,* (78" x 78" quilt), Mary Mashuta, 1992

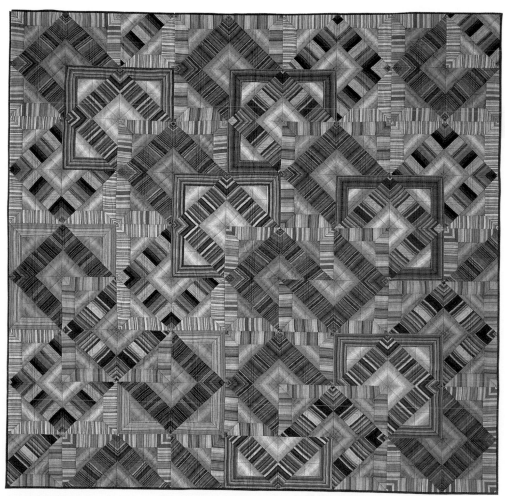

5.6 *Exploration: Learning to Get Along,* 71¹/2" x 69¹/2", Mary Mashuta, 1992

51

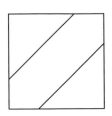

Cover Stripes block

5.7 Detail of Cover Stripes blocks[1]

5.8 *Country Crossroads*, 34½" x 34½", Mary Mashuta, 1995

▤ *X Blocks*

There are many X, or cross blocks which can show off your stripes nicely. Check with a viewing window to see whether your stripes look better in a perpendicular or horizontal placement.

Cover Stripes Block

I made up a very simple block named Cover Stripes while working with wearable art. The block has a diagonal bar and two equal triangles. The block is easy to piece, but amazingly, it can look very complicated because the units create a connecting pattern when joined.

Large X's are formed when numerous blocks are pieced together. You piece the blocks one way, but read the pattern another way. The pattern ends up looking bigger than what you started out with (5.7).

I tried the Cover Stripes blocks in two quilts, but limited the number of stripes used in each. It was fun seeing what I could do by using two colorways of the same stripe. Notice the hopscotch light/dark affect of the triangles behind my grid of stripes.

POSSIBILITY

5" Cover Stripes blocks = alternating, two-colorway stripe + light/dark triangles = grid (5.8)

POSSIBILITY

5" Cover Stripes blocks = alternating, two-colorway stripe + two-colorway print triangles = grid (5.9)

Interlocking X Block

I came up with the Interlocking X border for *Thinking of Janice* when I was sketching. Ruth Hayashi turned my border design into an all-over grid for her quilt. She proved that she could make a subtle Christmas quilt.

POSSIBILITY

Interlocking X block = dark/light stripe + dark print + wispy print triangles (5.10)

---

1. Pieced fabric for a garment and the cover of *Wearable Art for Real People* by Mary Mashuta (Lafayette, CA: C&T Publishing, 1989)

5.9 *Thinking of Janice,* 37" x 37", Mary Mashuta, 1995; in the collection of Elsie Peterson

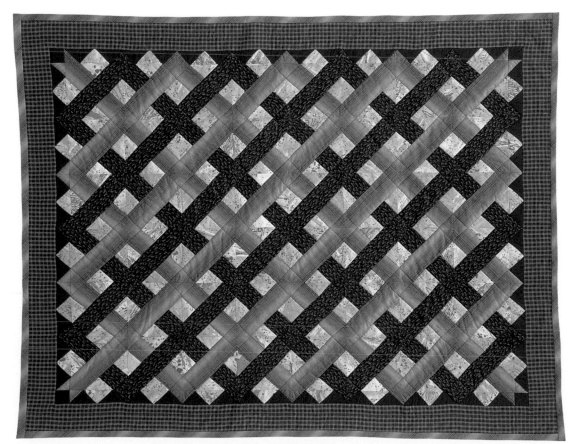

5.10 *Christmas Quilt,* 60" x 47", Ruth Hayashi, Berkeley, CA, 1995

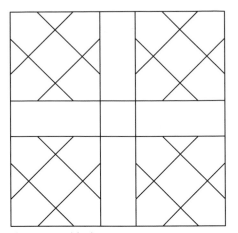

The Seasons block

Window X Block

Take portions of larger blocks to create a new block:
I took one segment of The Seasons block and made
Window X .

With the removal of the sashing between the blocks,
the adjoining blocks touch. If each block is made from
a different fabric, you read the blocks as you piece
them. However, when you make all of the blocks from
one fabric, you create a design that is read as floating
X's on a background. The new X's are formed when
four blocks meet.

POSSIBILITY

Window X block = small repeat, strong contrast stripe
+ light minor stripe background = X in a diamond
(floating X's if pattern continues) (5.11)

POSSIBILITY

Window X block = two-stripe blocks, adjoining blocks
flip flopped + dark print background = X in diamond
(floating X's if pattern continues) (5.12)

POSSIBILITY

Reverse the lights and darks and the same thing happens
(5.13).

Becky Keck picked a stripe with a large pattern
repeat and composed her quilt on a design wall. Since
she was making the quilt for her dentist brother, she
included a toothbrush fabric in the windows. The quilt
is fun because you can see the Window X blocks or
just the plain X's, depending on whether your eyes
focus on the print or the intersecting block corners.

5.11 One-stripe X

5.12 Two-stripe X

5.13 Two-stripe X

5.14 *Dental Daze*, 48" x 49", Becky Keck, Pleasant Hill, CA, 1992; in the collection of Dr. and Mrs. David Latz

POSSIBILITY

Window X block = large repeat stripe + conversation
print + minor stripe background triangles (5.14)

Elongated Window X Block
The proportions of an antique block helped me draw
an elongated version of Window X (5.15).

I first used the block in a garment. When the garment was stolen, I used the block as part of the design
for a mourning quilt on the next page.

5.15 Antique block

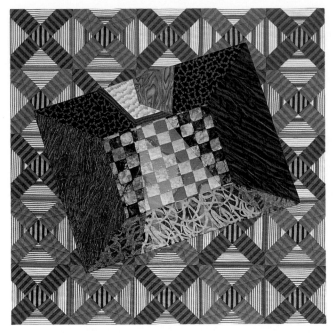

5.16 Detail of *Last Seen Wearing*, Mary Mashuta (quilt shown on page 86)

Nine Patch and Diagonal Cross Blocks

After I experimented with Window X, I found Nine Patch and Diagonal Cross blocks in a quilt search book. My block was alternated with a Nine Patch. The quilt was pieced in 1880s type scrap fabrics, but I knew it had great stripe potential. When a student shared a black and red-orange stripe with me, I knew I finally had a quilt for the Halloween fabrics I had been collecting for years.

POSSIBILITY

Nine Patch and Diagonal Cross blocks = one stripe X's with many values, orange negative-space triangles + conversation print Nine Patches in light/dark pattern (5.17)

Karen Dugas liked the appearance of my quilt and decided to try the pattern using a collection of 1930s reproduction prints she'd been amassing. To emphasize the '30s color palette, she alternated peach and '30s green fabrics within the negative spaces of her blocks.

POSSIBILITY

Elongated Window X = one stripe, two-colorway X's + multi-colorway negative space stripe triangles + one stripe centers (5.16)

POSSIBILITY

Nine Patch and Diagonal Cross blocks = one stripe X's with solid peach triangles + conversation print Nine Patches with solid green squares (5.18)

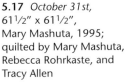

5.17 *October 31st,* 61¹/₂" x 61¹/₂", Mary Mashuta, 1995; quilted by Mary Mashuta, Rebecca Rohrkaste, and Tracy Allen

56

5.18 *Thirties Prints and Stripes*, 43" x 43", Karen Dugas, Pleasant Hill, CA, 1995

▦ *Grids*

The blocks I've been working with can be used to create all-over grids when you pay attention to what is happening in the positive and negative spaces.

Parallelogram Zigzag Grid

It is easy for me to get complex real quick, so I keep going back to a simple beginning idea. The Parallelogram Zigzag grid is drawn from a 4" square. Parallelograms and triangles form horizontal or vertical rows, depending on how they are colored.

POSSIBILITY

Two-colorway stripe parallelograms + two value triangles = set in horizontal light/dark rows = transparency (5.19)

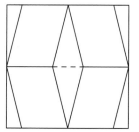

Parallelogram Zigzag (four blocks)

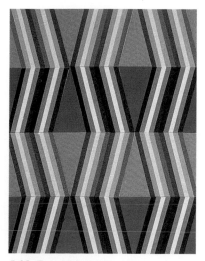

5.19 Transparency

I loved this pattern and decided to use Japanese fabrics from my collection to create something simple. Unfortunately, this was on my wall during the Oakland/Berkeley firestorm, so it turned into an abstract story quilt about the fire. It was one of the most exciting-to-make quilts I've ever created. (Because it was an important quilt, I made a decision to piece the design in diamonds rather than triangles, and it took a lot more time and skill to complete the quilt.)

POSSIBILITY

Assorted Japanese stripe, print, and air-brushed parallelograms + background diamonds = set in vertical rows + value change border (5.20)

The same design format was used for a small commissioned quilt. I picked a "soft," feathery, zigzag stripe to make *Alhambra Olé* and was determined to use all eight colorways of the pattern. If I hadn't been so "into" stripes, I would have never realized that the pattern was a stripe.

POSSIBILITY

Eight colorways zigzag stripe parallelograms + background triangles = set in vertical same color rows + darker border (quilt shown on page 4)

5.20 *Firestorm,* 73" x 83", Mary Mashuta, 1992

Zigzag Miter Block

Becky Keck liked my quilt *Firestorm*, but she couldn't remember exactly what my block looked like. She just knew that mine wouldn't be fun for her to sew together. Her block is a rectangle and has a miter. The rows are easy to join as long vertical rows.

POSSIBILITY

Assorted Japanese stripes in zigzag rows + background triangles = set in vertical rows (5.22)

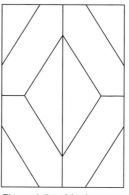

Zigzag Miter blocks

As Becky designed her quilt, she thought of her Michigan childhood and remembered the views of the autumn scenery seen through her window.

5.22 *Autumn Kaleidoscope*, 58½" x 72", Becky Keck, Pleasant Hill, CA, 1993

59

▤ *Continuous Designs*

The Patriotic Quilt block I adapted for *Coming to Terms* and *Lessons Learned* (page 17) was pieced as a continuous block. One unit continued into the next as it was sewn. Some continuous-looking blocks can actually be pieced as individual units, which makes sewing a lot easier and faster. Sue Arnold's quilt group, The No-Problem Quilters, discovered a block that fascinated them in a quilt calendar. They call it Snake Trail. It is a variation of the Bow Tie block.

As is their practice, a number of these women pieced their version of the quilt. Since Sue had taken my "Stripes" class, she was ready to visualize the quilt with a stripe in the two quarter-circle curved strips of the block. A wavy, marker-drawn stripe was a perfect choice for the curved strips. Also, the casual nature of the stripe meant she didn't have to be obsessive when trying to match chevrons.

POSSIBILITY

Snake Trail block = one color, marker-drawn stripe quarter-circle curved strips + many colorways "Pointillist Palette" negative space[2] (5.23)

Sue's striking black and white stripe pattern was also a many-colorway fabric that was designed by Nancy Crow for John Kaldor®. I purchased many of the colorways. Looking at Sue's quilt makes me want to get them out and play with this design. Quilt people designing fabric for quilters give us many design options to contemplate.

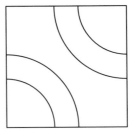

Snake Trail block

5.23 *Zebras Dancing in a Rainbow*, 52" x 52", Susan Maynard Arnold, Albany, CA, 1995

2. "Pointillist Palette" was designed by Debra Lunn and Michael Mrowka for Robert Kaufman Co., Inc.

Chapter 6

Discovering Other Stripe Blocks

I see quilt blocks everywhere that I could use with stripes; I just had to learn to "think" stripes. For example, you might see the Log Cabin pattern in this antique fabric, but I see a way of combining stripes.

Many blocks work well when pieced with stripes. I've included some blocks for you to try in this chapter. I have purposely included several quilts that use the same block; notice how the fabric choices make a difference.

▤ *Log Cabin Block*

Sooner or later, many quilters make at least one Log Cabin quilt. The block is a strong part of our quilting heritage. Traditionally, one half of the block is dark, the other half light. Blocks can be joined in many ways to create graphic, all-over patterns of dark and light. Nancy Taylor chose the Barn Raising set for her contemporary quilt.

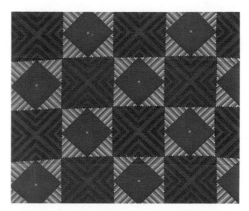

6.1 1880 cheater cloth in Log Cabin design

POSSIBILITY

Log Cabin blocks = assorted colorway, marker-drawn stripes and prints from collections for P&B Textiles by Jennifer Sampou (6.2)

6.2 *Log Cabin*, 35" x 35", Nancy Taylor, Pleasanton, CA, 1993

▤ *Sawtooth Block*

Lynn Crook is attracted to the Sawtooth block. *Razzle-Dazzle* is one of the quilts in Lynn's Sawtooth series. She always begins with a set of nine blocks. Lynn's design history with the block lets her see many possibilities within the Sawtooth design. She used many of the same stripes and prints that Nancy did, yet their quilts look quite different.

POSSIBILITY

Sawtooth blocks = nine blocks laid out in dark/light, diagonal bands (6.3)

6.3 *Razzle-Dazzle*, 64" x 64", Lynn J. Crook, Berkeley, CA, 1994; photo by Don Tuttle

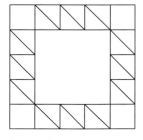

Sawtooth

▤ *Quick Basket Block*

I've always liked basket blocks. I invented the Quick Basket block when I was searching for an interesting, but less time-consuming block to combine with borders: Why spend time piecing when a large-scale print would do?

I soon ran into trouble with my fast and easy block. Traditional Basket blocks with handles have easy-to-see negative space around all four edges.

PROBLEM

Quick Basket blocks = large print triangles make it hard to distinguish the blocks from the border (6.4)

63

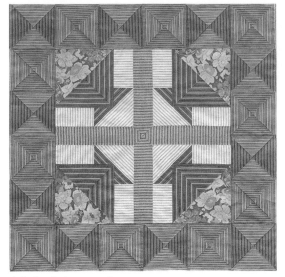

6.4 Confusing negative space

6.5 *Country Baskets*, 36" x 36", Mary Mashuta, 1995

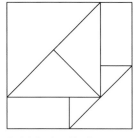

Quick Basket Block

SOLUTION

Quick Basket blocks = two contrasting borders + four-triangle square border (6.5)

SOLUTION

Quick Basket blocks = four-sided contrasting striped sashing + plain border + Streak of Lightning border (6.6 quilt shown on back cover)

SOLUTION

Quick Basket blocks = four-sided contrasting sashing + three-triangle square border (6.7)

6.7 *Floral Baskets*, 39¹/₂" x 40", Jane Schwarz, Pleasant Hill, CA, 1995

▤ *Star Blocks*

There are many star blocks which would adapt well to stripes.

Simple Star Block

As I look at the Simple Star block, I see that it has a hole in the center. The hole can be left as a square, or divided in many ways. The resulting blocks have many names, but I just call them Simple Star variations (A–E).

I tried putting stripes in the negative space of the Simple Star block. I was working with a spotty red-white-and-blue stripe and a colorful two-colorway, primary color print.

PROBLEM

Disaster = too much is going on (Variation C, 6.8)

SOLUTION

Remove outside print triangles + inset abstract ikat stripe squares = secondary pattern develops (6.9)

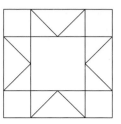

Simple Star block

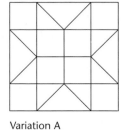

Variation A

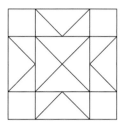

Variation B

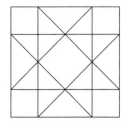

Variation C

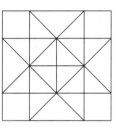

Variation D

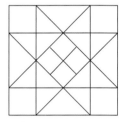

Variation E

6.8 Detail of *Wild Cats* work-in-progress, Mary Mashuta; photo by Mary Mashuta

6.9 Detail of *Wild Cats,* (47˝ x 47˝ quilt), Mary Mashuta, 1993

Jan Crum found another way to deal with cats. She used some pre-printed panels that contained Christmas cats.

POSSIBILITY

Simple Star block = stripe triangles + stripe negative space + Christmas cat block centers (6.10)

I decided to be more subtle in my second attempt at putting stripes in the negative space; the homespun stripes helped a lot.

POSSIBILITY

Divided center Simple Star block = rick-rack stripe + two colorways of medium and small-scale homespun stripes (Variation D, 6.11)

6.10 *Christmas Cats,* 64" x 64", Jan Shull Crum, Rodeo, CA, 1993

6.11 *Country Stars,* 48" x 48", Mary Mashuta, 1995

Star Lattice

I can get fancy with star blocks if I use my stripes wisely. If I put alternating Snowball blocks between my Simple Star blocks, I can create a lattice by placing stripes in all the triangles. What you see isn't what you start with.

The Star Lattice format is a wonderful showcase for special prints in your collection, or try creating an impressionistic view without using a colorwash design technique.

POSSIBILITY

Star Lattice = one-stripe triangles + secondary stripes to complete stars + conversation print (Variation B, 6.12)

POSSIBILITY

Star Lattice = similar stripe triangles + florals and abstract prints (6.13)

The big octagon in the Snowball block is a wonderful spot to showcase a feather wreath if quilting is your passion. This one was machine quilted.

POSSIBILITY

Star Lattice = one-stripe triangles + conversation prints (6.14)

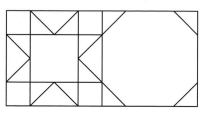

Simple Star block + Snowball block = Star Lattice

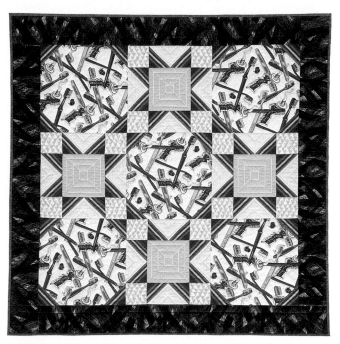

6.12 *Brush Often*, 42" x 42", Mary Mashuta, 1994; quilted by JoAnn Manning and Mary Mashuta

6.13 *Monet's Garden*, 42¹/₂" x 42¹/₂", Mary Mashuta, 1993; quilted by Rhondi Hindman and Mary Mashuta

6.14 *Victorian Dolls*, 48¹/₂" x 48¹/₂", Mary Mashuta, 1995; quilted by Rhondi Hindman and Mary Mashuta

6.23 Grandmother's Flower Garden blocks, Hope Hightower, Oakland, CA; in the collection of Peg Tetlow

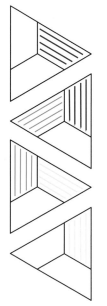

Forming Inner City sewing units

▤ *One-Shape Quilts*

Some quilts are based on one shape that is repeated over and over. Remember, you can do great things with simple shapes when you use striped fabrics.

Hexagons

Hope Hightower was one of the first quiltmaking teachers where I live. She enjoyed doing all of her work by hand, and she left an enormous stash of pieced Grandmother's Flower Garden blocks. I love them because they were made with striped fabrics. Hope certainly had fun playing and seeing what she could come up with (it seems as if quilters have used the hexagon shape forever). Here are some to enjoy.

POSSIBILITY

Hexagons + assorted stripes (6.23)

Inner City Block

After looking at hexagons, you might say that the Inner City block is made up of divided hexagons. Actually the basic unit is classified as a trapezoid (four-sided figure with two parallel sides). The Inner City block is another example of "what you see" is not "what you did." The "T" shapes are composed as inter-meshing units on the design wall. When it is time to sew, trapezoids from these touching units are joined to form a triangle. Then the triangles become rows.

Marilyn Henrion shows us how effectively stripes can be used in the Inner City design. She is used to dealing with small pieces of fabric because, for many years, she worked at the Fashion Institute in New York City and collected the discarded fabric samples.

POSSIBILITY

Inner City block = assorted stripes + many chevrons (6.24)

Marilyn created "soft" chevrons of stripes in her all-over design. (Most often chevrons occur at right angle miters.) Note that sometimes the stripes match and sometimes they don't. This makes for a less rigid design.

Mitered Rectangle Block

The Mitered Rectangle block has much in common with the Inner City block. Both are made from trapezoids: Inner City blocks have three chevrons per unit and Mitered Rectangle blocks have two. However, the chevrons are "soft" in the former and are at a right angle in the latter block.

Anne Ito became fascinated with the Mitered Rectangle block. She searched through her collection of Japanese fabrics and was able to use many woven stripe fabrics to construct the blocks for *Kaidan* (the English translation of her quilt name is "steps").

POSSIBILITY

5" x 9" Mitered Rectangle = Japanese stripes and solids + blocks staggered on the diagonal (6.25)

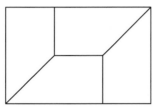

Mitered rectangle block

6.24 Detail of *An Immense Journey*, 63" x 63", © Marilyn Henrion, 1993; photo by Karen Bell

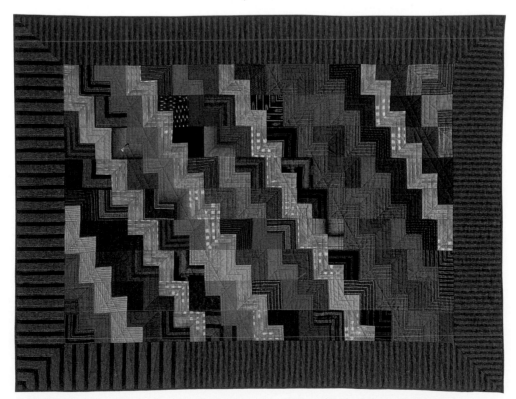

6.25 *Kaidan, 76" x 59"*, Naoko Anne Ito, Berkeley, CA, 1995; quilted by Rebecca Rohrkaste

71

Triangles

No shape could be more quilt-like than a triangle. Marilyn Henrion pieced many triangles together to make *Brighton Beach Memories*. (It is fun to figure out how she pieced this quilt.)

POSSIBILITY

Triangles = assorted stripes (6.26)

I enjoy Marilyn's stripe collection. Although they vary in scale, most have very simple pattern repeats. Note that all of the stripes contain white, but only one or two other colors.

Marilyn leads tours of the New York City Garment District. Let me tell you, Marilyn knows where to find stripes!

6.26 *Brighton Beach Memories*, 45" x 52", © Marilyn Henrion, 1995; photo by Karen Bell

Chapter 7

Stripes in the Sashing, Borders, and Binding

Sashing joins the quilt blocks; the borders complete and/or complement the quilt design (or just plain make the quilt bigger); and the binding finishes the edges of the quilt. Stripes make a difference in all of them.

▤ Sashing

Sashing holds blocks together physically and separates them optically. Stripes make your quilt sashing more interesting: they can calm your quilt down or liven it up.

Print Sashing with Striped Blocks

If you are concentrating on stripes in your quilt blocks, you may want to put a print in the sashing instead. You can always put stripes in the sashing posts.

POSSIBILITY

Print sashing with four-triangle pieced stripe posts (7.1)

POSSIBILITY

Embellished print sashing with pieced stripe post (7.2)

7.1 Detail of *Mosaic Star,* George Taylor (quilt shown on page 68)

7.2 Detail of *Trick or Treat,* Mary Mashuta (quilt shown on page 69)

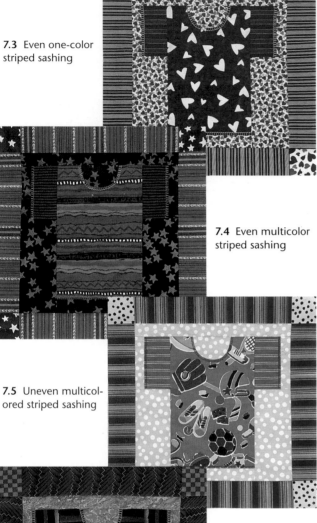

7.3 Even one-color striped sashing

7.4 Even multicolor striped sashing

7.5 Uneven multicolored striped sashing

7.6 Zigzag striped sashing

Simple Striped Sashing

I did a series of T-shirt blocks for a magazine article. Note how the selection of the stripe sashing complements the T-shirt in each block. (Also note the background fabrics and the corner posts.)

POSSIBILITIES

- Even one-color striped sashing (7.3)
- Even multicolored striped sashing (7.4)
- Uneven striped multicolored sashing (7.5)
- Zigzag striped sashing (7.6)

Stripes can bleed into your block color when they touch and match. Notice that my yellow stripe is a shade of yellow, rather than an exact color match.

POSSIBILITY

Uneven, contemporary, multicolored striped sashing (7.7)

It is important where you place the yellow in striped sashing if the lines are large and prominent because the yellow immediately becomes the focus. I could have placed my yellow band dead-center to engage the eye, but I purposely moved it around to keep the design flowing.

POSSIBILITY

Uneven, contemporary, multicolored border striped sashing (7.8)

7.7 Uneven, contemporary, multicolored striped sashing

7.8 Contemporary border striped sashing

Remember that stripes look great as bias cuts. My T-shirt project gave me an opportunity to use up ten over-dyed, bias-cut stripes.

POSSIBILITY

Bias-cut, over-dyed, black-and-white striped sashing (7.9)

Pieced Striped Sashing

If you want something more complicated than just plain sashing, play with the sashing pieces and the adjoining blocks and see what happens.

FRIENDSHIP STAR SASHING

You can dress up your sashing and posts by adding triangles to the posts, and then turning them into a Friendship Star sashing. You can either place your stripes in the sashing or in the stars.

POSSIBILITY

Striped sashing + Friendship Star posts (7.10)

POSSIBILITY

Print sashing + Friendship Star posts with striped triangles (7.11)

7.9 Detail of *One Size: Assorted Colors* (57" x 71" quilt), Mary Mashuta, 1994

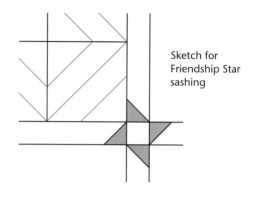

Sketch for Friendship Star sashing

7.10 *Hearts and Hands,* 24" x 24", Mary Mashuta, 1994; in the collection of Hearts and Hands, Tokyo, Japan

7.11 *Quilt Show,* 56" x 56", Mary Mashuta, 1992

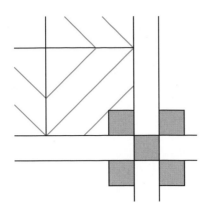

Sketch for Nine-Patch sashing

7.12 Detail of *Huntington Beach: 1955,* Mary Mashuta (quilt shown on page 85)

7.13 Detail of *Memories of Christmas Past*, Mary Mashuta (quilt shown on page 28)

NINE-PATCH SASHING

I doodled with a Quilter's Surprise block to come up with my Friendship Star sashing. I realized that the corner triangle of the block could be broken down further. By placing a square in the triangle, I came up with Nine-Patch sashing.

POSSIBILITY

Add Nine-Patch sashing to Quilter's Surprise block (7.12)

Divide Sashing into Blocks

If you piece a stripe sashing, the design gets more complex. To decide how large to make the sashing blocks, or units, just divide your original block into equal segments. For example, a 16" block makes four equal 4" units.

POSSIBILITY

Cover Stripes block makes Zigzag sashing (7.13)

▤ *Borders*

Many quilters claim a quilt isn't done until a border is added. While I find this is not true for all quilts, a border is a good addition to many quilts. Like a picture frame on a painting, an appropriate border can complete, contain, and complement a quilt. The simplest borders are created by joining strips of plain or printed fabric to the edges of a quilt. While this practice is acceptable and adequate, I find it far more interesting to go a step further and come up with a more challenging border.

Stripes can be used very effectively to create borders. They don't have to be complex to be interesting, either. As always, make the stripes work for you. Stripes make the borders look more complicated than they really are. And, even though I am emphasizing pieced stripe quilts in this book, please realize that non-stripe quilts may also benefit from a striped border.

Picking a basic border design is important, but you'll have to also figure out how to get around the four corners. Sometimes all that is needed is a miter. Often, an additional block will do. Or, you can create a device, or special block, to get around the corner. If all else fails, just use a plain block.

Print Borders

You may love large-scale decorator prints, but may not have found a place for them in your quilts yet. Try featuring them in a border, and add a pieced corner block.

POSSIBILITY

Decorator print + pieced stripe and plaid corner blocks (7.14)

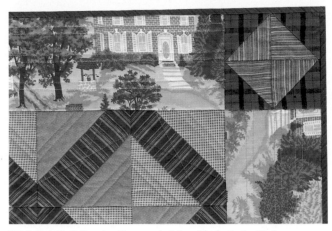

7.14 Detail of *Country Crossroads*, Mary Mashuta (quilt shown on page 52)

I have always loved toilé fabrics (two-color printed French scenes). Yet, the motifs are large and don't easily lend themselves to being cut into smaller bits. They are the most beautiful when you are able to see a lot of fabric at once. I finally realized they could be used as a border, as long as the strips weren't mitered.

POSSIBILITY

Toilé border piece + pieced corner block (7.15)

7.15 Detail of *Tejas Toilé,* Mary Mashuta (quilt shown on page 68)

7.16 Detail of *Blue Snake Trail* #1 (74" x 84" quilt), Rebecca Rohrkaste, Berkeley, CA, 1995

7.17 Detail of *a.pa.ini?*, Joan Capron Helm (quilt shown on page 33)

7.18 Detail of *Log Cabin*, Nancy Taylor (quilt shown on page 62)

Simple Stripe Borders

A stripe border can stop the action at the edge of a quilt.

POSSIBILITY

Busy scrap quilt center + narrow stripe inner border + plain outer border (7.16)

It is interesting when borders relate to the design of the inner quilt—especially when borders extend the action to the edge of the quilt. Stripes are perfect candidates for simple borders, and they reinforce other stripes that are used elsewhere in the quilt.

Joan Helm had already used a black-and-white stripe as a background for batik greeting card pictures. She selected a similar, but huge, stripe to frame her quilt. Joan used a small print "coping strip," or border, to separate the stripes in the center of the quilt from the larger border stripe. Mathematically, this also assured that her corner miters would end up in the right place.

POSSIBILITY

Large scale stripe + coping strip (7.17)

Nancy Taylor finished her Log Cabin quilt with a plain striped border. To set the border apart, she selected a colorway not used in her Log Cabin blocks. To liven things up, she added print corner blocks and appliquéd leftover logs in a random design.

POSSIBILITY

Plain stripe + appliquéd helter-skelter strips + unpieced corner blocks (7.18)

Simple Pieced Striped Borders

You don't have to work as hard as you may think to add a striped border, just work with what's already happening in your quilt. Jan Crum added a small-scale Christmas border stripe to her star quilt. To keep it from being boring, she added triangle insets. (She knew she could use same-fabric insets as long as she changed the direction of the stripes.) She marked off the midpoints of her stars and placed the insets there.

POSSIBILITY

Christmas border stripe + two-triangle, mitered insets + mitered corners (7.19)

Christine Davis' original block was set on point, which meant she ended up with half-blocks at the edge. This is where she placed "completing" half triangles in her striped border. (She made her black-and-white stripes look more complicated because she added a border print to one edge.) Further festiveness was added by placing twirling Pinwheels in the corner blocks.

POSSIBILITY

Striped triangle set in perpendicular-cut striped border + twirling, pieced stripe corners (7.20)

Even contemporary art quilts can have striped borders. Nancy Meyer extended the inner design field of her quilt by intersecting two simple striped borders with print fabrics. Originally, both stripes were cut parallel and then mitered at the corners. However, the quilt composition became much more interesting when the inner border was changed to a perpendicular cut. The double border worked effectively to both expand and contain Nancy's composition.

POSSIBILITY

Inner + outer border + change of direction in similar stripes (7.21)

7.19 Detail of *Christmas Cats*, Jan Shull Crum (quilt shown on page 66)

7.20 Detail of *Victoriana*, Christine Davis (quilt shown on page 43)

7.21 Detail of *Take Time to Smell the Flowers* (55" x 55" quilt), Nancy Meyer, Plymouth, MI, 1992

79

7.22 Detail of *Dental Daze,* Becky Keck (quilt shown on page 55)

7.23 Detail of *Thinking of Janice*, Mary Mashuta (quilt shown on page 53)

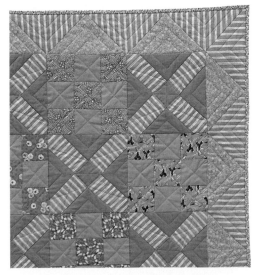

7.24 Detail of *Thirties Prints and Stripe*, Karen Dugas (quilt shown on page 57)

Pieced Striped Borders

If you want a pieced striped border, try adapting a very simple block. Repeating striped multiples will make it look more complicated than it is.

COVER STRIPES BORDER

There aren't many blocks simpler than Cover Stripes. It makes good sashing, but it also makes a great border.

POSSIBILITY

Alternating light/dark (two stripes) blocks + subtle stripe negative space + special corner miter block (7.22)

INTERTWINING X BORDER

I crossed the diagonal of the Cover Stripes block and ended up with an Intertwining X. If you are using an interconnecting block, you will have to plan how to get around the corner so the transition is optically continuous. If the transition doesn't work, try inserting a plain block in the corner, and consider it a corner post!

POSSIBILITY

Intertwining X inner border = two-colorway, one-stripe interweave + embellished, two-colorway, one-stripe outer border.

While you are looking at *Thinking of Janice*, also note that I embellished the plain, striped outer border with buttons and raw-edge appliquéd X's to make it more playful (7.23).

Triangle Striped Borders

Triangles look great pieced in stripes. Effective borders can be created by selecting shapes, like triangles, from your quilt block pattern, or just beginning with triangles the size of your quilt block. Since the new piece relates to your block size, the math work is kept to a minimum. Draw it out on graph paper to scale, and use viewing windows.

SIMPLE TRIANGLE BORDER

Nothing could be simpler. Karen Dugas began with her 7½" block and used that measurement for the hypotenuse of her triangle. It is easy to chevron around the corner with striped triangles on the outside.

POSSIBILITY

One-stripe triangles cut perpendicular to the hypotenuse + print triangles (7.24)

STREAK OF LIGHTNING BORDER

Streak of Lightning is a slightly more advanced border that uses triangles. One set of triangles is cut perpendicular to the hypotenuse, and the other is cut parallel. The two triangles can be cut from one or two stripes. If you use two stripes, just keep the stripes in the same color range.

POSSIBILITY

Streak of Lightning border = one stripe triangles (one parallel, one perpendicular) + swirl print (7.25)

POSSIBILITY

Streak of Lightning border = two same-color stripes (one medium scale cut parallel and one small scale cut perpendicular) + a contrasting negative space stripe (7.26)

THREE-TRIANGLE SQUARE BORDER

Here's a great looking, very simple border that can also be dimensional. Note how it winds around the corner. All you do is divide your square into two triangles, and then divide one of those in half again.

POSSIBILITY

Three-triangle square border = one large stripe triangle + two small triangles (one small scale stripe + print) (7.27)

POSSIBILITY

Three-triangle square border = one large stripe triangle + two colorways of one stripe for two small triangles (7.28)

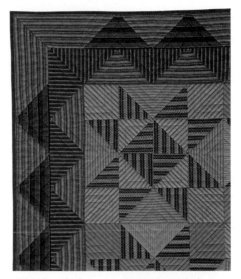

7.25 Detail of *Teddy Bear Mosaic* (30" x 30" quilt), Mary Mashuta, 1995

7.26 Detail of *Country Stars*, Mary Mashuta (quilt shown on page 66)

7.27 Detail of *Pansy Baskets,* work-in-progress, Mary Mashuta

7.28 Detail of *Christmas Shirt*, Mary Mashuta (quilt shown on page 27)

7.29 Four-triangle square border

7.30 Four-triangle double square border

7.31 Four-triangle square woven border

FOUR-TRIANGLE SQUARE BORDER

Since I'm talking about triangles, I should remind you that any square can be divided into triangles. Simply divide your block measurement into even increments, draft a square, and then divide the squares into triangles.

POSSIBILITY

5" four-triangle square border = two stripes + blocks rotated (7.29)

POSSIBILITY

4" four-triangle double square border = stripe with conversation print + blocks rotated (7.30)

Cutting your stripes perpendicular to the base creates a woven border as the stripes from the adjoining blocks touch and chevron.

POSSIBILITY

Four-triangle square woven border = cut mirror image triangles if it is impossible to flip and use the other side of the fabric (7.31)

STRIPE SQUARE AND TRIANGLE BORDERS

Also experiment with a Square and Triangle border. To calculate sizes, divide your quilt measurement into easy divisions. Add a "coping" strip, or inner border, if you need to separate the border from the blocks, or if your measurement isn't quite right.

I have used Square and Triangle borders for a class exercise and have seen the most unusual combinations of stripes being put together—and ending up working well in the design. Even though I am good at visualizing, I can't always anticipate a result. Experimentation is essential.

Several beginning decisions have to be made when using a Square and Triangle border:

First, select two stripes (one for the squares and one for the triangles).

Second, make sure there is contrast in color, value, and scale in the two fabrics (try to avoid having the design elements bleed together).

Third, decide the orientation of the stripes in the squares and triangles (use a viewing window).

Finally, plan ahead how to get around the corner!

At the end of the chapter I have included a set of seamless templates so you can create your own set of glued mock-ups.

POSSIBILITY

Corner = square + small miter + one large triangle and one half-triangle (7.32)

POSSIBILITY

Corner = square + small miter + two-trapezoid miter (7.33)

POSSIBILITY

Corner = two squares with miter + large triangle miter (7.34)

POSSIBILITY

Corner = square + two small miters (7.35)

POSSIBILITY

Corner = square + four small miters (7.36)

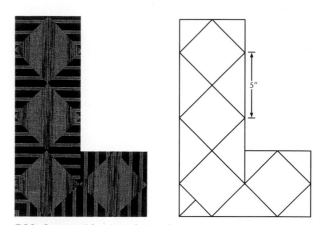

7.32 Corner with mitered triangles

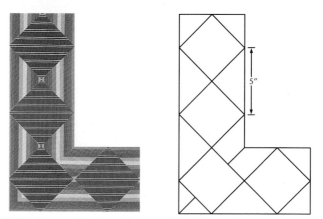

7.33 Corner with mitered trapezoids and triangles

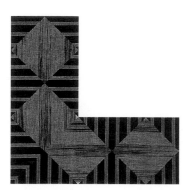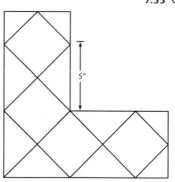

7.34 Corner with mitered squares

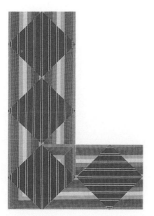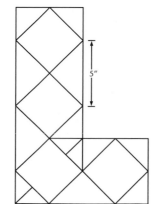

7.35 Corner with two-triangle miters

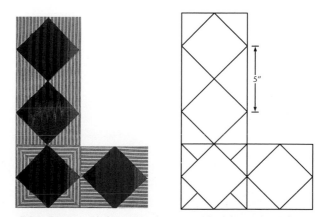

7.36 Corner with four-triangle miters; block by Kathy Galo

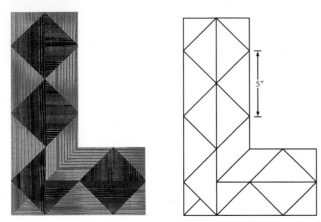

7.37 Two-triangle square variation; block by Angie Woolman

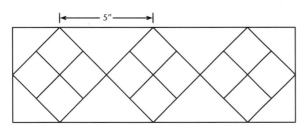

7.38 Four-square variation

STRIPE SQUARE AND TRIANGLE BORDER VARIATIONS

Given the basic square and triangle format, many variations are possible because the square can be divided.

POSSIBILITY

Two-triangle square variation = change direction of stripes in triangles (7.37)

The square could also be divided into four squares (or triangles).

POSSIBILITY

Four-square woven variation = stripes parallel to edge of squares (7.38)

POSSIBILITY

Four-square Pinwheel variation = stripes diagonal to corners of square, light/dark stripes (7.39)

POSSIBILITY

Four-square Bull's Eye variation = stripes diagonal to corners of square, stripes matched (7.40)

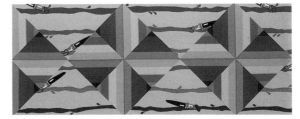

7.39 Four-square Pinwheel variation

7.40 Four-square Bull's Eye variation

Askew Set Borders

For a change of pace, I began experimenting by designing quilts with an askew set. To form an askew set, first start with a square then tip, or "float," the square within a larger square. Doodling with a pencil and graph paper will help you work out your design options.

POSSIBILITY

Askew set = pieced square + floated checkerboard square (7.41)

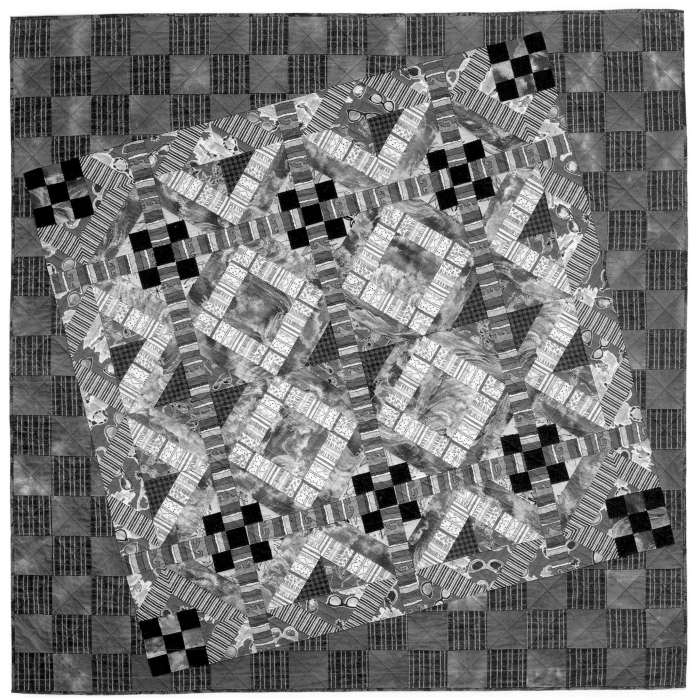

7.41 *Huntington Beach: 1955, 68" x 67¹/2", Mary Mashuta, 1993*

For *Last Seen Wearing,* I went through the askew process twice.

POSSIBILITY

Askew set = pieced view of room + pieced grid + pieced checkerboard (7.42)

When I'm designing an askew set, I never piece an entire top and then cut a whole in it. Before I start constructing, I've already sketched on the graph paper how big my center square will be, and then I leave a space for it. (It's important, however, to also have a little extra fabric left around the hole when you trim off your actual hole size plus seam allowances).

7.42 *Last Seen Wearing,* 55" x 55", Mary Mashuta, 1994

PROBLEM

Askew set = insetting square in another square requires careful planning

Or, rather than fussing with an inset square, you might find it easier to just add four large triangle border pieces to the design instead. (If I had added a small border to *Huntington Beach: 1955,* I could have added a border of this type.)

SOLUTION

Askew set = add four triangles to a square

I used pieced triangle squares in my large askew triangles. I cut the triangles from a batik stripe that I purchased in South Africa. The batik process made the lines somewhat abstract and irregular looking, and I knew the design of the fabric would look wonderful when it was cut into pieces. The beauty of this fabric is that it isn't "perfect."

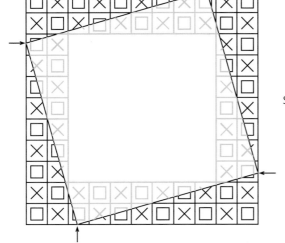

Sketch of an askew set

7.43
Dawn for a New Day, 77" x 77",
Mary Mashuta,
1993

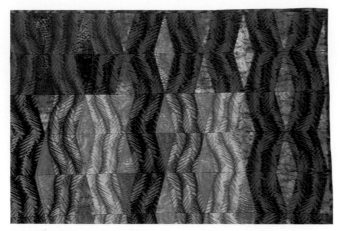

7.44 Detail of *Alhambra Olé* border, Mary Mashuta (quilt shown on page 4)

7.45 Detail of *Firestorm* border, Mary Mashuta (quilt shown on page 58)

Two different stripes can also work beautifully in an askew set border (see *Tourist in the Gourmet Ghetto* quilt on page 28).

An askew set requires more time and an intermediate skill level. If you have both and would like your quilts to look more complex, give the askew set a try!

Color Change Borders

When I made *Alhambra Olé,* I wanted to include eight colorways of my striped fabric, so placing some of the darker value colors in a border was natural.

POSSIBILITY

Stripe color change border = darker values of stripes create an optical border (7.44)

The *Firestorm* quilt doesn't have a striped border. However, I used a change of colors to set the striped interior apart from the border area. The parallelogram and diamond pattern pieces continue unabated to the quilt edges (7.45).

▤ *Bindings*

Binding is one of the last steps in completing your quilt. Your attitude may be "let's get this done so I can 'gift-it' or put it in the quilt show," but careful consideration of the binding can really make a difference. Binding does more than finish off the edge of your quilt: it is an opportunity to calm down or enliven the activity level of your quilt. Stripes make great binding. And they can be used whether or not stripes are used in the rest of the quilt. In terms of design impact, the calmest stripe bindings are cut perpendicular and have low value contrast; the wildest stripe bindings are cut diagonally and have high value contrast.

Browse back through the book and look specifically for the striped bindings. Cover the binding of a photographed quilt with plain paper (to mask the binding), and see what the quilt looks like without it. Now remove the paper and note the visual impact of the binding!

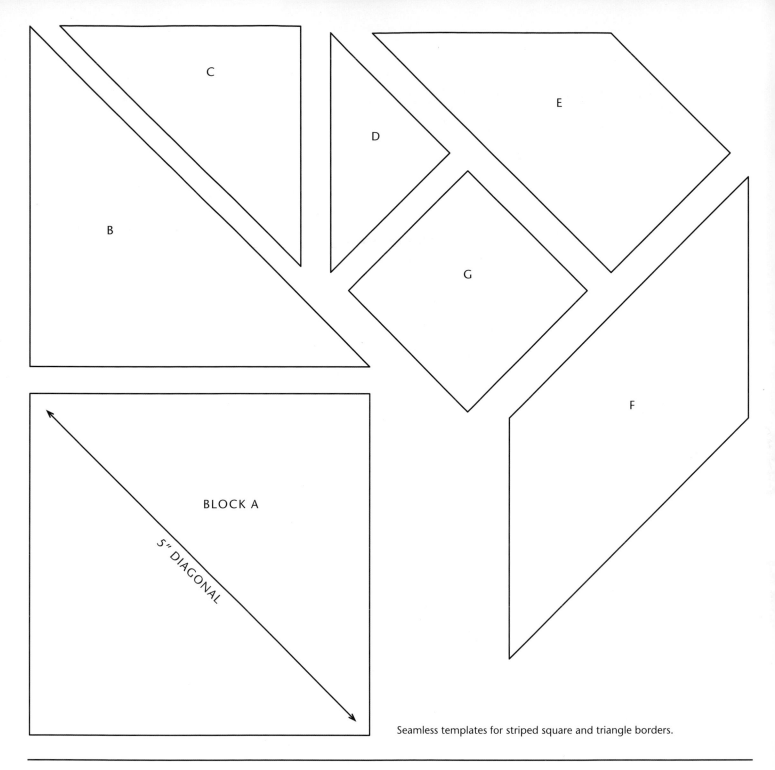

C

B

D

E

G

F

BLOCK A

5" DIAGONAL

Seamless templates for striped square and triangle borders.

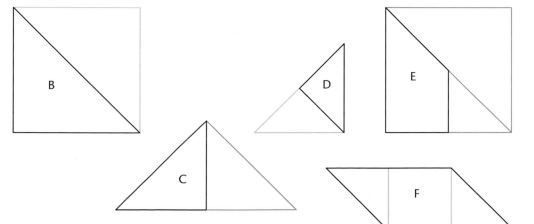

B

C

D

E

F

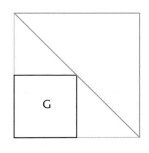

G

Chapter 8

Machine Quilting Stripe Quilts

Quilting does more than hold the parts of the quilt together: it adds to our aesthetic enjoyment of the quilt. Although I love beautiful hand quilting, out of necessity I have had to learn to quilt by machine. And somewhere along the way, I discovered that machine-quilted stitches show better on striped fabrics. In this last chapter, I want to share some of my other discoveries as well, which might make quilting easier for you. Because students are always asking me how I get my quilts so flat, I have even added pointers at the end of the quilting discussion on how to ensure a flat quilt.

▤ Deciding How to Quilt a Stripe Quilt

The quilting stitch helps bring the quilt design to life! My quilting patterns are straightforward and reinforce the linear pattern of my stripes. I use a combination of stitch-in-the-ditch quilting with straight-line quilting. When the quilt is finished, some of my quilting shows, while the rest is only noticeable at close range. When the quilt is turned over, however, there is a consistent pattern of coverage. As a bonus, having an equal amount of stitching in all parts of the quilt helps to ensure a flat end product.

Even though I am eager to start the decorative stitching, I take the time to grid the blocks and the individual pieces (within each block) with stitch-in-the-ditch quilting. This is boring, tedious work, but there is no way to get around it. I stitch each piece right next to the seam line. This causes the quilt to lie flat and makes it easier to add my decorative quilting. I usually use monofilament thread for this first step, since it shows very little after the whole quilt is done. I piece with 12 stitches to the inch, but it isn't necessary to use such a small stitch for stitching-in-the-ditch. Moving the stitch selector to get about 10 stitches to the inch moves the work through the machine much faster.

Many quilters use variations of the meandering stitch to machine quilt quickly. For meander stitching, an all-over pattern is created by making loops and squiggles in an ongoing, freeform, continuous line. Stopping and starting are minimal and a lot of territory is covered in a short amount of time. Meander stitching does not enhance the lines in stripes, however. Use it to fill in printed or solid areas, but don't meander too densely or it distorts the more lightly stitched areas. Before you know it, you will be adding more straight-line stitching to try to balance things out!

▤ *Straight-Line Machine Quilting*

Stripes are a linear type of pattern. Straight-line machine quilting reinforces and complements the linear pattern of stripes. You can stitch right on top of stripe lines, you can stitch perpendicular to stripe lines, and you can stitch diagonally across stripe lines. Basically, I let the fabric "talk" to me. Many of the design possibilities come to me while I am doing my basic stitch-in-the-ditch drudge work.

I pick straight-line stitching patterns that are easy on the eye. For example, it might be very difficult to consistently stitch on top of a very small line; whereas, a big bold, high-contrast line becomes an easy target for the machine needle. Straight-line quilting enhances a striped quilt, but it is more time consuming than meander quilting. Plan ahead and see how long you can continue a line of quilting. I don't mark a whole quilt before I quilt it, I mark it as I go along. I have to stop to make pivoting turns, but the needle down position and the knee lift (if you have either of these on your machine) makes this fast and easy. I have accepted that I have to stop and start more often than with meander stitching.

Strategies for Straight-Line Quilting

To keep my quilting line straight, I have learned to sew beside a piece of masking tape or to use the edge of the walking foot as a guide. I sew at a constant, moderate speed. "Haste makes waste" is a good maxim to remember. Most of my designs can be marked off with pins at crucial points, such as midpoints on the block or pieced seams. The middle of a stripe may be an obvious midpoint, but other times, you will have to measure to find the midpoint. (Remember that blocks are often smaller after stitching, so measure the whole distance and divide by two.)

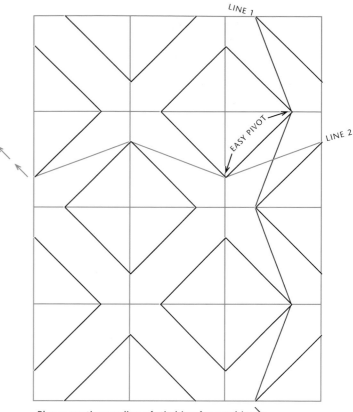

Plan a continuous line of stitching for machine quilting (note the easy pivots)

You may have always marked your quilting lines with pencil or chalk. I prefer to use masking tape because there is no tell-tale evidence left once the quilting is finished. I use ¼" or ¾" tape, and reuse the tape several times. A fresh piece of tape may be too strong for more delicate fabrics so always test on a sample first. Also make sure you have fairly new tape, since old tape can leave a sticky residue. Finally, never leave the tape on the quilt. Apply, stitch, and then remove it.

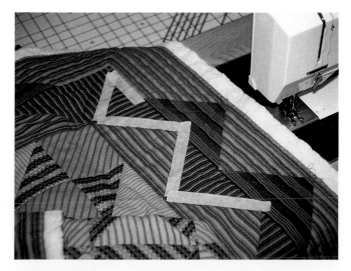

8.1 Use masking tape as a stitch guide for straight stitch quilting; photo by Mary Mashuta

After I have pinned my midpoint, or pivoting points, I run tape from point to point. I only tape small areas at a time, preferring to prepare just as much area as I will stitch between starting and stopping my line of thread. (Many design lines have two starting and stopping places because it is impossible to completely rotate a block around as is done in hand quilting with a hoop.)

To make your task flow more evenly, try the following tips: Learn to sew beside the tape, not on it. I clean off any tape residue that may have built up on the needle by running my fingers down the needle from top to bottom. If you have trouble with the tape sticking to the underside of your walking foot, make sure you cut the tape longer than the distance spanned by your stitching line. This helps to keep the ends of the tape from getting caught on the underside of the walking foot.

As you sew, be alert to changes in stitch size. If all of a sudden you are getting small stitches, stop and check to see if the tape has caught on the underside of the walking foot. Since I always sew with a needle-down position on my machine, I can lift the presser foot to check and not lose my place. Sometimes all that is needed is for you to raise and then lower the attachment.

As previously mentioned, I use monofilament thread to stitch in the ditch. Monofilament doesn't add color, so after any showy threads are added, it tends to go unnoticed. I select a neutral color for the bobbin thread and decrease the tension to help to hide the loops on the top side. (If a 5 setting is normal, lower the tension to a 4, which is looser.)

When I want my quilting stitches to show, I do my decorative straight-line machine quilting with Sulky® rayon thread. Rayon is lustrous and easy to work with, but to show off the luster, it is necessary to use a long stitch length. Eight or nine stitches per inch shows off the thread. The longer stitches are adequately strong, and, again, the machine work is faster. Rayon thread comes in a full-color palette so it is easy to find colors that complement your quilt. Often I use a number of colors in the same piece. Let the fabric or the mood of the quilt give you a hint. I usually pick a neutral bobbin thread but sometimes I match the rayon color. (It doesn't bother me if there is more than one color of thread on the back of the quilt.)

I am also attracted to multicolored rayon threads. However, the color change occurs over a long length if you are straight-line stitching; as opposed to decorative stitching which uses up a lot of thread. (I did use a high contrast orange and black rayon in *Firestorm* and a lower contrast blue and white rayon in the tie-dye area of *Dawn for a New Day*.) Sue Arnold cross-hatch quilted the background of her quilt with multicolored rayon thread.

Sometimes it is appropriate to use metallic threads. Multicolored metallics are often less contrasting than

8.2 *Detail of Zebras Dancing in a Rainbow,* Sue Maynard Arnold (quilt shown on page 60)

multicolored rayon threads. I place the spool in a small jar and lower the tension (as is common practice when using monofilament thread). I also add Sewer's Aid to the spool occasionally to ease the flow of the thread through the machine. Two beads down the side of the spool are sufficient.

I use a Sharps Size 12 needle (occasionally a 10 is necessary) to sew monofilament and rayon thread. It has a sharper point than a universal needle and this makes for straighter stitching lines. The new embroidery needles are great for metallics because they have a larger eye, but I don't find them necessary for rayon.

Examples of Straight-Line Machine Quilting

The straight-line quilting designs I select are easy and straightforward. They are determined by the block patterns and the stripes used, and some are more complex than others. The amount of quilting in a specific quilt is partially influenced by the size of the blocks. A larger version of a block requires more quilting to look good and to be adequately quilted. Remember, some quilts are made for real use and will be washed; others are made as decorative pieces. Some quilts are more important to me than others, so my feelings vary over the amount of time and effort I want to invest in quilting them.

Let's look at some close-up quilt details so you can get ideas for straight-line quilting designs.

PROBLEM

You don't know what to do. (Learn to go with what's there.)

SOLUTIONS

• Follow shapes of pattern pieces (8.3).
• Cross at midpoints (8.4).
• Start on striped lines and continue across a print area (8.5).

PROBLEM

What should you do in plain areas?

SOLUTIONS

• Use block measurements to section off an area (8.6).
• If quilting looks skimpy, add a second line of stitching (detail of quilt shown on page 77).

8.3 Detail of *Yulara: Journey to the Red Center,* Mary Mashuta (quilt shown on page 47)

8.4 Detail of *Animal Parade,* Mary Mashuta (quilt shown on page 50)

8.5 Detail of *Wild Cats* (47" x 47" quilt), Mary Mashuta, 1993

8.6 Detail of *Tejas Toilé* , Mary Mashuta (quilt shown on page 68)

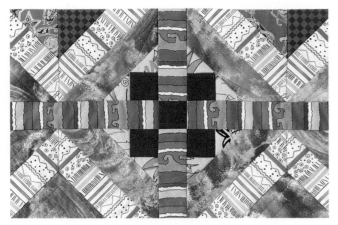

8.7 Detail of *Huntington Beach: 1955,* Mary Mashuta (quilt shown on page 85)

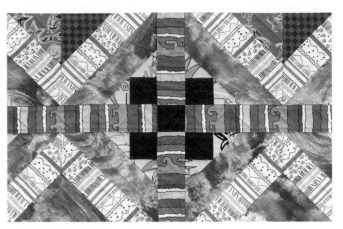

8.8 Detail of *Huntington Beach: 1955*

8.9 Detail of *Firestorm,* Mary Mashuta (quilt shown on page 58)

8.10 Detail of *Tourist in the Gourmet Ghetto,* Mary Mashuta (quilt shown on page 28)

8.12 Detail of *Victorian Dolls*, Mary Mashuta (quilt shown on page 67)

8.13 Detail of *Victorian Dolls*

PROBLEM

Not enough quilting (8.7)

SOLUTION

Add more stitching (8.8)

PROBLEM

Tired of straight stripes and straight stitching lines?

SOLUTIONS

- Add curved stitching to contrast the straight stitching (8.9).
- Add meander stitching with perle cotton and buttons (8.10).
- Add a cable border (8.11).
- Add a feather wreath to a plain area (8.12).

PROBLEM

Feather wreath not large enough to fill area

SOLUTION

Add more straight lines (8.13)!

8.11 Detail of *Country Baskets,* Mary Mashuta (quilt shown on back cover)

▤ *Ensuring a Flat Quilt*

I like flat, even quilts so I always follow the same procedure when I machine quilt so my end product will be as flat as possible. I press often, I pay attention to batt selection, I use a walking foot, and I put lots of quilting stitches in my pieces. Creating machine quilting stitches that look good takes practice. What I do does take time, but I am happy with the results.

Because I have a home economics background, I was taught to press as I sew. In addition to pressing during construction, I also give a final touch-up press before the top is basted. This pays off in the end because it makes machine quilting easier. After the quilt has been entirely quilted, I also take the time to press it again. (Remember to match the iron setting to the fiber content of your batt!) Pressing helps to relax any distortions and neaten things up. I then let the quilt rest overnight on my design wall, or other flat surface, before binding it.

I baste my quilts on the top of my worktable. A mat, which is grided 36" x 68", helps me to line the quilt up squarely. (Quilts larger than this are worked in sections.) I have a 60" metal ruler (available at lumber yards or hardware stores) to lay across the quilt top so the blocks in rows can be patted into place. When things are evened out, I safety-pin baste approximately every 4". Getting a friend to help makes basting a much faster process.

Selecting the Batt

Batt selection also makes a difference in how flat a quilt is. I usually select cotton/polyester blend batts because they make a flatter end product than polyester batts. I do occasionally use low-loft polyester batt for the baby quilts, such as *Animal Parade* (quilt shown on page 50).

Many people skimp on the quilting stitches when they machine quilt. My quilts have a lot of quilting in them, but certainly not as much as the folks who enjoy stippling. To create a flat quilt, I have found it is important to have the same amount of quilting consistently over the whole surface. The monofilament stitching doesn't show graphically in the end, but when I turn the quilt to the back side, I see a consistent pattern of stitching lines that are made up of the stitching-in-the-ditch and decorative stitching.

▤ *Conclusion*

I love stripes, and I can't get enough of them. My imagination is filled with ideas for new quilts to make with striped fabric, but it has not always been this way. When I started quilting, it was hard for me to understand why some quilters specialized in creating only one type of quilt: I wanted to try each new type I encountered. Now I know that the more you narrow your focus, the more you see in that aspect of quilting. My journey with stripes has progressed from a tentative first use to a place where I now experience an excited anticipation toward each new project in which I can use stripes. I hope this book and the quilts in it have made you more aware of stripes and their potential use in quilts. May the next fabric you purchase be a striped one, and may the next quilt you make contain at least one stripe.

About the Author

Mary Mashuta sees stripes all around her: in nature, on buildings, in home furnishings, on the clothes in her closet. Everywhere she goes, she looks for stripes. Her studio and her quilt room (the room where her quilts live) are loaded with striped fabrics waiting to be used.

Mary first explored the possibilities of stripes in her wearable art, and then broadened the scope to include stripes in her quilts. One of the nicest compliments Mary ever received was from an art student taking a class, "You think in fabric, just like my sculpture teacher thinks in stone." Now Mary has learned to think in stripes.

A quiltmaker since the early 1970s, she is a professionally trained teacher and has taught on the national quiltmaking circuit since 1985. She is the author of *Wearable Art for Real People* and *Story Quilts: Telling Your Tale in Fabric*. Her informative articles on wearables, story quilts, quilter's workspaces, and stripes have appeared in *Quilter's Newsletter Magazine*, *American Quilter*, *Lady's Circle Patchwork Quilts*, and *Threads*.

Other Fine Books From C&T Publishing:

An Amish Adventure - 2nd Edition, Roberta Horton
The Art of Silk Ribbon Embroidery, Judith Baker Montano
Basic Seminole Patchwork, Cheryl Greider Bradkin
Beyond the Horizon, Small Landscape Appliqué, Valerie Hearder
Buttonhole Stitch Appliqué, Jean Wells
Colors Changing Hue, Yvonne Porcella
Dating Quilts: From 1600 to the Present, A Quick and Easy Reference, Helen Kelley
Elegant Stitches: An Illustrated Stitch Guide & Source Book of Inspiration, Judith Baker Montano
Everything Flowers, Quilts from the Garden, Jean and Valori Wells
The Fabric Makes the Quilt, Roberta Horton
Faces & Places, Images in Appliqué, Charlotte Warr Andersen
Heirloom Machine Quilting, Harriet Hargrave
Impressionist Quilts, Gai Perry
Mariner's Compass Quilts, New Directions, Judy Mathieson
Nancy Crow: Improvisational Quilts, Nancy Crow
The New Sampler Quilt, Diana Leone
Paper Cuts and Plenty, Vol. III of Baltimore Beauties and Beyond, Elly Sienkiewicz
Patchwork Quilts Made Easy, Jean Wells (co-published with Rodale Press, Inc.)
Quilts for Fabric Lovers, Alex Anderson
Quilts, Quilts, and More Quilts! Diana McClun and Laura Nownes
Schoolhouse Appliqué: Reverse Techniques and More, Charlotte Patera
Small Scale Quiltmaking: Precision, Proportion, and Detail, Sally Collins
Soft-Edge Piecing, Jinny Beyer
Tradition with a Twist: Variations on Your Favorite Quilts, Blanche Young and Dalene Young Stone
Trapunto by Machine, Hari Walner
The Visual Dance: Creating Spectacular Quilts, Joen Wolfrom

For more information write for a free catalog from:
C&T Publishing
P.O. Box 1456
Lafayette, CA 94549
(1-800-284-1114)